T0290527

Interpreting Naval History at Museums and Historic Sites

INTERPRETING HISTORY

About the Series

The American Association for State and Local History publishes the Interpreting History series in order to provide expert, in-depth guidance in interpretation for history professionals at museums and historic sites. The books are intended to help practitioners expand their interpretation to be more inclusive of the range of American history.

Books in this series help readers:
- quickly learn about the questions surrounding a specific topic,
- introduce them to the challenges of interpreting this part of history, and
- highlight best practice examples of how interpretation has been done by different organizations.

They enable institutions to place their interpretative efforts into a larger context, despite each having a specific and often localized mission. These books serve as quick references to practical considerations, further research, and historical information.

Titles in the Series

Interpreting Native American History and Culture at Museums and Historic Sites by Raney Bench
Interpreting the Prohibition Era at Museums and Historic Sites by Jason D. Lantzer
Interpreting African American History and Culture at Museums and Historic Sites by Max van Balgooy
Interpreting LGBT History at Museums and Historic Sites by Susan Ferentinos
Interpreting Slavery at Museums and Historic Sites by Kristin L. Gallas and James DeWolf Perry
Interpreting Food at Museums and Historic Sites by Michelle Moon
Interpreting Difficult History at Museums and Historic Sites by Julia Rose
Interpreting American Military History at Museums and Historic Sites by Marc K. Blackburn
Interpreting Naval History at Museums and Historic Sites by Benjamin J. Hruska

Interpreting Naval History at Museums and Historic Sites

Benjamin J. Hruska

ROWMAN & LITTLEFIELD
Lanham • Boulder • New York • London

Published by Rowman & Littlefield
A wholly owned subsidary of The Rowman & Littlefield Publishing Group, Inc.
4501 Forbes Boulevard, Suite 200, Lanham, Maryland 20706
www.rowman.com

Unit A, Whitacre Mews, 26-34 Stannary Street, London SE11 4AB

British Library Cataloguing in Publication Information Available

Library of Congress Cataloging-in-Publication Data

Names: Hruska, Benjamin J., author.
Title: Interpreting naval history at museums and historic sites / Benjamin J. Hruska.
Description: Lanham : Rowman & Littlefield [2016] | Series: Interpreting history ; 9 |
    Includes bibliographical references and index.
Identifiers: LCCN 2016025196 (print) | LCCN 2016028523 (ebook) | ISBN 9781442263673
    (cloth : alkaline paper) | ISBN 9781442263680 (paperback : alkaline paper) |
    ISBN 9781442263697 (Electronic)
Subjects: LCSH: United States—History, Naval. | United States—History, Local. |
    Historic sites—Interpretive programs—United States. | Historical museums—United
    States. | War memorials—United States.
Classification: LCC E182 .I189 2016 (print) | LCC E182 (ebook) | DDC 359.00973—dc23

Printed in the United States of America

Dedicated to Dr. John Allen Gable

1943–2005

Historian, Mentor, and Friend

Contents

Preface

I N MAY 2012, after completing my ninety-three-thousand-word history dissertation at Arizona State University (ASU) on a group of World War II sailors who survived the sinking of their vessel, I wanted a break from history and all naval topics. Over the course of four years, I researched the intersection of American naval veterans, public military memorials, and a group of World War II sailors from a U.S. Navy escort carrier called the USS *Block Island*. Besides graduate work at ASU, I visited government archives in Washington, D.C., interviewed individual veterans, and attended ship's reunions across the nation. On many perfect afternoons for desert golfing, I buckled down writing in the Hayden Library or in a coffee shop. Thus, to celebrate the completion of my naval dissertation, I sought an experience well outside the bounds of anything related to closing an archive or library.

After graduation, a friend drove me to California. Traveling down a two-lane dirt road, we approached a large metal fence extending to the eastern and western horizons. As the dirt road expanded into a large turnaround area, we reached our goal: the Mexican border. Hugging my friend goodbye and carrying a backpack full of outdoor supplies, food, and water, I started my trek north into the desert on the Pacific Crest Trail (PCT). The PCT is a 2,700-mile hiking trail meandering over the deserts and mountain ranges of California, Oregon, and Washington, ending at the Canadian border. My goal for two months of hiking was to cover the driest section, to complete the first eight hundred miles over a range of desert ecosystems. My daily agenda consisted of walking twenty to thirty miles, stuffing down as many calories as possible, and sleeping. No reading photocopies of World War II battle reports, eating from vending machines in basement archives, or editing for hours, fueled by caffeine.

Walking north into the desert and encountering a rattlesnake warming itself on the trail before seeing a fellow hiker, my thoughts centered on water, in particular, the location of the next place for obtaining drinking water. At times in the first section of the trail, which is the lowest, hottest, and driest, the next source of drinking water can be forty miles away. Hauling seven liters of water granted a personal lesson in the weight of water, which is 2.2 pounds per liter, meaning I carried fifteen pounds of water to safely reach the next water supply. While I was successful in escaping thoughts of seawater, I was unable to avoid naval history; even in crossing the largest desert region in North America, surrounded by the majestic Joshua tree and scorpions of the Mohave, naval history existed.

Six hundred miles into my hike, I came to a barren section of road on California Highway 187. Here at Walker Pass, I stood with my thumb exposed, pointing upward, seeking a ride to the nearest town to resupply. Hitchhiking is an introduction into Daoism. There is no real point in being in a hurry because on an isolated road a friendly driver may materialize in the next minute or in the next three hours. Today I was in luck, as the second vehicle climbing up the pass saw me; the driver slammed on the brakes and stopped nearby. Two Native American gentlemen pulled up in a twenty-five-year-old SUV. My spot in the back seat, amid a scattering of alfalfa and straw, seemed appropriate with how I smelled after the eighty-five miles I had traversed since my last shower. We cruised down into the desert basin to the east, at times traveling up to ninety miles per hour. With my anticipation rising for a shower and a nondehydrated hot meal, I saw a highway advertisement in a blur beside the road noting a U.S. Navy base. Nearing the desert city of Ridgecrest, it became quite clear by the numerous civic and business signs that this desolate outpost revolved around a naval base called China Lake.

Of the two days scheduled in Ridgecrest for letting my battered feet heal, washing sweat and sand from clothing, and resupplying my ration of dehydrated mash potatoes and instant coffee, I witnessed the amalgamation of a small desert community and a naval base larger than Rhode Island. As the primary facility of weapons testing, officially known as Naval Air Weapons Station China Lake, this location in the shadow of the Sierra Nevada mountain range has been instrumental not only in weapons development for the U.S. Navy, but also engine testing, computing theory and development, and submarine design. In short, this is a Navy town.

After befriending a retired engineer who grew up and spent his working career as a government engineer at the base over a cup of coffee, the engineer volunteered to serve as my docent in touring the base and explaining its history. Cruising the base in his Suburban, he explained its growth starting from the time his father worked there at the peak of the Cold War. In showing me the naval base, he dissected his own career as an engineer, which included working on perfecting the ejector seat and also a practice called reverse engineering. The latter practice included disassembling a Mig fighter plane flown to the West by a defecting Soviet pilot. With the parched environs surrounding the fenced base, the concept of the ocean itself seemed a world away. However, his naval tales included President John F. Kennedy visiting and witnessing a weapons display of naval firepower on the bombing range. All his stories demonstrated the interwoven relationship China Lake had with the U.S. Navy during the Cold War and beyond.

This experience challenged my perception of naval history. While popular history books gravitate to the naval engagements at sea, much of naval history takes place on land. Whether it is the basic training of sailors, education of officers, or construction of vessels, navies materialize in the minds of men and shipbuilding facilities on land. In addition, when touring China Lake, one sees the memorialization of individual sailors, weapons systems, and vessels commemorated in a host of ways on land. Retired aircraft lined up along streets, names on buildings, and statues around the base all sought to memorialize China Lake's naval history. This reframing of my view of what is naval, and the forms of memorialization, whether that be in the museum or in a public space, is the driving force behind the text that follows.

CHAPTER 1

Leaving Port

An Introduction

Public History

As a graduate student with professional museum experience before entering a PhD program, I encountered being classified as a "public historian." For a few singularly academic-minded professors, public history equated with projects and conference papers weak in theory and methodology. In short, it was believed we produced less challenging versions of scholarship in comparison with true academic history that is rich in theory and esoteric lingo. I luckily encountered, and latched onto, a number of academic professors who recognized the strengths of public history and persuaded them to join my dissertation committee. However, with the other graduate students, the undertone persisted that we were somehow the less challenged body of students. We challenged the norm of limiting our learning to the classroom, library, or archive. In addition, we spent summers completing internships in Washington, D.C., researched and wrote site histories for the National Park Service, and attended conferences and presented papers with other "public historians," many of whom had no random sets of letters after their names pointing to an advanced degree.

In discussions with graduate school friends on both sides of our graduate program, the main difference between the two groupings did not result from dealing with the public, but rather the perceived notion that public historians avoided sinking their teeth into the deep theoretical abyss of such scholars as Hegel, Weber, and Marx. The argument went that public history equated to shallow history. Our papers and exhibits simply stated the facts. Or as one of our public history professors succinctly quipped with the warning, "Just one damn fact after another." And to be honest, we have all encountered such public history products, just like we all have encountered a bad meal. Poor examples such as these can lead to the charge that public historians produce only "happy history," exhibits or books that do not challenge and ask larger questions, such as which groups are underrepresented in political processes, civic engagement, and local history. For example, a historical society in a small town displays a dated exhibit on the wonders of their founders with a laser-like focus on rich white Anglo-Saxon males and exclude all other members of society. While examples of these dated forms of history still exist as relics in local historical societies, their academic cousins, such as a military history from the 1930s that incorporates the same aforementioned exclusions, remain in dark corners of university library systems. Collecting dust on the back shelves of libraries, histories written in the nineteenth and the first half of the twentieth centuries also demonstrate that at one time academic histories of the Western world also excluded large segments of the population. Whether generals or admirals, governors or presidents, or a range of men of industry, in the past both academic and public historians can trace a genealogy to the one-dimensional view of the past that excludes a cross section of societies, including immigrant groups, women, and the enlisted ranks of military service.

This being said, I found that my time working with academic historians dramatically and greatly improved my initial dissertation study. Pushing me beyond just conducting oral histories with U.S. Navy servicemen, the academic classroom challenged me to add additional dimensions of inquiry, such as: How does the commemoration of war take place? Who controls this story formation of the remembrance of wars? What can we learn from the differing versions of memorials from one produced by veterans to that of one built under the direction of a government? These and other questions resulted from my experience at ASU. After a feeling-out process, students of both types learned that far from paradoxical, both fields sought the same goal, the only difference being a question of audience. While poor examples of both public and academic history abound, for public historians ours is more visible, and thus a larger target for criticism. As for naval topics, a top-down approach to the past has proliferated in seeking to shape the narrative with one specific admiral or famous battle. However, we as public historians of naval history owe it to the thousands of other sailors, and their families, to ask larger questions to represent both the depth and breadth of historical inquiry.

Naval topics challenge the idea that history only resides within the terrestrial boundaries of the nation—that oceans do not have histories. Historical investigations centered on land miss the impact of the world's oceans on human development. The scholar Rainer F. Buschmann cautions against an overconsideration of land. He writes, "practitioners often unwittingly conceived of oceans as vast empty liquid spaces that obstructed rather than furthered human development."[1] Other recent scholars in this vein address this issue in a collection of essays. In *Sea Changes: Historicizing the Ocean*, the authors "take issue with the cultural myth that the ocean is outside and beyond history, that the interminable, repetitive cycle of the sea obliterates memory."[2] Likewise, public historians of naval topics must challenge the notion that history ends at the beach or the dock from which vessels sail into conflict.

For naval topics, one major obstacle is that there is no fixed point to serve as a platform of memory because most events take place on the open seas. Subsequently, naval veterans themselves invented unique ways of commemorating that were complex and multiform and outside the bounds of the traditional land-based method of the erection of a stone monument to function as the site for a ceremonial event. For example, embracing museums, naval veterans sought to anchor artifacts related to their wartime experiences. Actions such as these in this work demonstrate the evolution of different points of view with naval topics and highlight the contested nature of remembering all naval conflicts, whether the lens is with fleets, entire navies, or even nations. Embracing this contested nature, which can seem daunting in the short term, invites long-term successes.

Subject and Scope

Naval history transcends the relatively recent manmade inventions of nation-state boundaries. This fact harmonizes with a recent development of a "global" perspective in AP History courses and university lecture halls viewing bodies of water as uniting peoples as opposed to dividing them. Across language groups, eras of technological development, and cultures, a close examination of the human relationship with waterways highlights these as gateways to change rather than roadblocks. In this narrative, waterways are defined as any oceans, seas, rivers, or other bodies of freshwater encountered in the course of human history. This definition takes into account the fluid nature of waterways, in which rivers, seashores, and lakes are always in flux. Mirroring human history, the boundaries of water are constantly in motion.

Naval traditions are proudly centered on the heritage of a vast range of societies, as seen in Britain's global impact with the Royal Navy or the Maori voyage of discovery and colonization of New Zealand around 1100 CE. Naval traditions transcend nearly all categories of place, culture, and scale. Inquiry from a naval perspective incorporates all continents, language groupings, and religious traditions. Most societies at some point in their history, whether at the Battle of Salamis in classical Greek history or with the Imperial Chinese Navy under the Shang Dynasty, embrace and celebrate their naval heritage.

An examination of these forms of remembrance, including museums, national memorials, and public ceremonies, highlights the formation of these modes of commemoration. Likewise, geography will play a factor as many of these sites reside on coastlines, river valleys, freshwater ponds and lakes, or even riverbeds empty of water most months of the year. In addition, landlocked sites can also commemorate naval topics with connections made to an individual vessel, a particular crewmember, or a link to the name of vessel due to the christening of a ship after the name of a city, region, or indigenous tribe. The scope of this work attempts to demonstrate both the depth and breadth of naval interpretation with global examples serving as a window into the subject matter.

Theory

Public historians must explore the relationship between history and memory. These two words are often used interchangeably, and without careful consideration of the true meaning of each

Figure 1.1. At the entrance gate of the Naval Air Weapons Station–China Lake, naval history on display in the Mojave desert. Photo by Ben Hruska.

term, we will miss the strong theoretical underpinning required of all historians. The scholar Pierre Nora's article "Les Lieux de Memoire" argues that the words *history* and *memory* differ in a number of important ways. He writes, "Memory and history, far from being synonymous, appear now to be in fundamental opposition."[3] By this, Nora argues that history is a construction of the past attempting to sum up all that took place in a given frame of reference. This construction of history is required to purge variety from individual and group stories in order to produce a single narrative giving meaning to a certain group, state, or nation. He writes, "History's goal and ambition is not to exalt but to annihilate what has in reality taken place."[4] These constructions of history, Nora argues, must discard most memories to manufacture one overarching narrative.

Pierre Nora addresses the experience of memory for the individual who undergoes it. He writes, "Memory is a perpetually actual phenomenon, a bond tying us to the eternal present."[5] The act of memory does not occur in the past, but the present. This argument that memory takes place in the present forces the museum professional to consider the effects of later events on memory. Memories develop and transform over time as the actual event producing the memory recedes into the past. The complexities of this notion are compounded for collective memory. As years pass, not only will the collective memories change, but the means of recalling the memories will also alter. This is exemplified by the explosion of possibilities with methods of summoning memory ushered in with the digital age, such as oral histories, YouTube clips, and online genealogical research. Memorial activities and groups devoted to the collective memory are not stagnant entities, but transform over time as these drift further into the future from the event that spawned them.

Nora specifically describes the role of collective memory and veteran groups. He describes these groups as being "dedicated to preserving an incommunicable experience that would disappear along with those who shared it."[6] Collective memories, Nora argues, are all endangered, no matter the number of individuals involved. He also suggests that the longevity of history over memory is partially the result of each term's point of reference. According to him, "Memory attaches itself to sites, whereas history attaches itself to events."[7] If his suggestion is true, that memory is attached to sites, how does this affect historical events formed devoid of land? If collective naval memories develop in a place that cannot be visited in a traditional sense, such as on the sea, what manifestations occur? Collective naval memories will materialize in places that will not allow the placing of a stone marker, the laying of a stationary wreath, or the opening of an exhibition. Naval historians do not have the luxury of those interpreting land battles. While these naval histories can recall the body of water that fleets moved over, public historians must develop other methods and techniques for interpreting naval history that occurred on the open ocean.

Historiography

In a short discussion of the historiography of naval history, it is important to understand the design of this book, with four areas of naval interpretation. We will consider examples in the widest possible range of scale, production, timeframe, and geographic location. For example, we will consider a British-built aircraft carrier currently operating in the Indian Navy that will be converted into a floating museum by the Indian government, and at the same time examine handmade memorialization of naval experiences by World War II–era U.S. Navy sailors in suburban Arizona. We will push the boundaries of naval interpretation in examining methods including oral histories and model building, even using Legos. In our exploration of naval topics, we will throw the widest possible net and see what we haul in.

A quick point is needed on these four areas, as they are not mutually exclusive. For example, the four themes being commemoration, objects, exhibition, and public memorials could all in theory occur at the very same time and location. Or another combination of the four could occur at a ship-based museum, a ceremony honoring past sailors, or the commissioning of a new war vessel. These themes are rarely siloed completely in any interpretation of history, as a statue in a park can exhibit and memorialize simultaneously. However, for this study, dividing these concepts into four areas will allow us to explore the true depth of naval interpretation while realizing that these themes can feed off each other and enhance the overall interpretation goals. Thus, with the broadest approach to understanding historical examples, this work will look for a combination of innovative approaches, successful traditional methods, and both sea- and land-based methodologies of naval interpretation.

Commemoration

Lacking a land-based site to memorialize sea battles and navies, naval interpreters over the centuries have developed other means of commemoration. For this work, memorialization is defined as any means or action aimed at recalling or remembering any naval topic. Broadly defined memorialization could include the naming of streets, stone markers in cathedrals, and national war memorials. While many memorialization examples are found in public spaces, it is important to note that grassroots naval memorialization is seen in the barrooms of American Legions or in veteran's homes. Engineering goals of these invented memorials include creating meaning for individuals, families, ship's company, or nation-states. Similarly, products of naval commemoration can include individual ship models, reunions of sailors and their family members, or the commissioning of a painting.

Objects

The University of Alaska's Museum of the North, located in Fairbanks, defines the word *accessioning* as "the process of creating a permanent record of an object, assemblage, or received from one source at one time for which the Museum has custody, right, title."[8] This definition stresses not only protecting the physical object once it is donated, but also the creation of a "permanent record" about the object. As someone who can say this with experience, curating a maritime exhibition with objects is a wonderful experience, especially if all the objects retain detailed information about what and who used them. A sword fishing harpoon in an exhibition holds much more significance if pertinent information on an object exists. For example, who used this? Do we have an image of the owner? When was this used? Is the harpoon directly related to any other object in the collection? All aspects, if woven correctly, bring objects to life with a human connection and shed light on the subject of sword fishing. For the average modern-day visitor who only looks at the ocean as a place of recreation with surfing or hitting golf balls off a cruise ship, naval objects contain the power to open a door to the past in which young boys fought from the Royal Navy's masted vessels, hunted whales in the South Pacific, or fished for cod in wooden boats hundreds of miles from land. Objects hold special power in invoking meaning for naval topics such as sea battles, time of service, and loss at sea, and the forthcoming chapter on objects will probe all these methods.

While we will explore numerous uses of objects by individuals, ship's crew, and nations, a unique mode for naval history is the preservation of a former war vessel. For example, the oldest commissioned preserved ship of war is the HMS *Victory*, which still serves as a memorial to the Royal Navy's victory at the 1805 Battle of Trafalgar and, in a larger context, that of the Georgian Navy. Saving and maintaining a ship, if done correctly, is one of the most impressive feats any organization devoted to historical preservation can accomplish. However, the pitfalls, including underestimating required funding, workload, and scale of project, are enormous. Thus, this section will cover the uses and challenges of objects in a range of naval topics, including the very tempting and costly challenge of accessioning a former war vessel into a museum collection.

Exhibitions

Methods of naval exhibition vary just as much as the methods of man fighting on the oceans. A quick survey of the exhibitions of the United States National Naval Aviation Museum in Pensacola, Florida, demonstrates the methods used by curators in interpreting naval warfare in a land-based museum setting, such as the use of a single artifact, collection of objects, or the construction and display of naval models. Pulling into the parking lot, in front of the museum rests a fifteen-foot-high, thirty-thousand-pound anchor from the USS *Antietam*, CV 36, granting a window into the scale of vessels involved in carrier aviation. Entering the museum, visitors witness another curatorial method: over a dozen handcrafted aircraft carrier models demonstrate the evolution in design from the pioneering USS *Langley*, CV 1, to the modern-day nuclear-powered Nimitz class aircraft carrier. For museum professionals, these models demonstrate periodization, breaking up carrier aviation into bite-sized chunks to show change over time. A tour of the south wing reveals naval objects used in a larger exhibition, such as the World War I exhibit looking at the first large-scale use of naval aviation in the history of warfare. All three of these exhibitions utilize objects to bring needed context and interpret the curatorial themes.

A full visit to the National Naval Aviation Museum requires days. Exhibition examples include a cutaway of a PBY Catalina showing the plane's many hidden compartments, explore Bob Hope's USO shows on board ships, art galleries honoring the U.S. Navy and her sailors, and visitors look up seventy-five feet in the air to see a formation of former U.S. Navy Blue Angels hanging near the ceiling.[9] All these methods, encapsulated in one museum, highlight the historiography of naval exhibitions. In the upcoming exhibitions chapter, with a diverse use in terms of geography, topics, and methodology, we will explore successes in exhibiting the long relationship of man and the sea.

Public Memorials

The dedication of public memorials to those lost and those that survived transforms a space into something sacred. Whether in a place of worship or a municipal park, naval memorials offer a terrestrial location for remembrance that in most instances is critically lacking for recalling loss at sea. Unlike land battles that retain a natural location for the placement of memorials, naval topics are more problematic. Lack of a natural specific site for the erection of a stone marker, flagpole, or gathering of attendees requires more inventive forms. This chapter will demonstrate the lengths individuals will go to in seeking closure with past trauma and honoring victims. Additionally, naval memorials mirror a ship at sea in completing a number of different functions at the same time.

For example, naval memorials converted from a decommissioned aircraft carrier, besides hosting naval reunions to honor deceased shipmates, can also include educational touchtanks for young visitors to learn about what marine life residing in the seawater surrounding a preserved vessel. A naval vessel is compartmentalized, with small sealed interlocking rooms conducting a host of functions simultaneously, such as the tasks of loading bombs on aircraft, baking bread, and providing sleeping quarters. So too with decommissioned war vessels transformed into public memorials. At the longstanding Nautical Nights Overnight Program at Battleship Cove in Fall River, Massachusetts, youngsters and their parents are allowed to sleep on board a World War II–era battleship. Over the course of a full day, this program encapsulates life on board ship, including eating meals in the Officer's Wardroom and speaking with individual veterans about their naval service.[10] Public programs on floating ship-based memorials demonstrate the range of options in engaging the public, either in holding a traditional formal commemoration or facilitating an engaging educational activity granting greater meaning to a memorial.

Challenges in Naval History

Location

Historians of naval themes need to first and foremost reconsider the meaning of place. Naval vessels are kinetic, designed and constructed to move over the largest portion of the earth's surface: the oceans. Thus, in framing naval topics, it is important to remember that our subject by its very nature is one of movement. Thus, lacking a terrestrial land-based location for most naval actions, veterans, nations, and navies invent methods of remembering events that took place on the open ocean. An additional factor is that most vessels, after being deemed obsolete, are scrapped and no longer exist in the physical form. Thus, naval topics welcome creative means to recall the past. We inherit a great deal of creative latitude in developing memorials and exhibitions.

Saltwater

There is no separation of saltwater from naval history. While anomalies did take place, such as the freshwater Battle of Lake Erie in the War of 1812, saltwater is a part of the stories we tell. Beyond the symbolic metaphors, this fact has a huge impact on the practical side of things. Saltwater is tough on men and vessels. Steel hulls, wooden masts, and the youngest and ablest of sailors all break down relatively quickly with exposure to saltwater. Thus, ships of war, without consistent maintenance, literally fall apart in a couple of decades. For preservationists of retired vessels, this concept is only exacerbated with saltwater and sea air rapidly deteriorating artifacts. From metal tools to navigational charts made from paper, conditions of the sea take their toll on all and thus shape the methods public historians must employ.

Technology

For the modern viewer, walking on board a masted sailing vessel composed of wood, metal, lines, and sail, it is easy for thoughts to drift toward romantic notions of the past. We must always be on guard for nostalgia, such as the excitement and drama of the novels of C. S. Forester's Horatio Hornblower, because we risk overlooking that the eighteenth-century sailors experienced the same emotions as modern-day warriors, those of terror, loss, homesickness, and levels of fear beyond words. In addition, with sentimentality it is easy to forget that masted war vessels from the age of sail are examples of technological prowess. Be it a U.S. Navy Vietnam–era Swift boat patrolling rivers, a fifteenth-century caravel of the Portuguese Empire, or a Chinese junk from the Song Dynasty, all these illustrations exemplify state-of-the-art technology for the societies that produced them.

Technological innovations from any society, whether in sail design or nuclear propulsion, are quickly adopted for military purposes. Thus, in interpreting a single ship we can view a vessel as an ever-evolving ambassador to new technologies. This notion is exacerbated with the rapid transformation in communication, propulsion, and weapons since the Industrial Revolution. Thus, this work will consider techniques employed by the USS *Midway* Museum in San Diego, which interprets an aircraft carrier with a career spanning nearly fifty years. Commissioned at the very end of World War II and serving into the First Gulf War, her current curators addressed interpreting multiple generations of communication systems, computing power in navigation, and demographics of sailors, which after 1978 included female sailors, in a single space. Done correctly, curators can embrace not only telling multiple stories, but also exhibits that shed light into the evolving technologies seen in the lifespan of vessels.

Famous Engagements

Another consideration for naval warfare is how it differs with land engagements. For museum professionals, the most noted disparity is the condition of the site of battle once the guns have gone silent. Land battles leave a plethora of war material and victims, all things that can be collected immediately or even centuries later and used in interpreting the site. Naval warfare is a different animal. As noted naval historian James Hornfischer wrote, "When a ship sinks, the battlefield goes away."[11] All debris, including broken bodies, ripped sails, or fuel oil, with the currents and tides of the sea, quickly dissipate any small trace of the engagement. Public historians, when interpreting famous engagements such as the Royal Navy's finest hour at the Battle of Trafalgar, will not only face the challenge of the site being on the open ocean, but also the lack of artifacts in comparison with major land battles.

Memorial Placement

The major conundrum for naval memorials is placement. Naval feats occur at sea, thus the traditional etched stone markers at Gettysburg, Culloden, and Somme will not apply. Engagements taking place hundreds, if not thousands, of miles from land, coordinates on a map essentially, present the issue of historic stability. Public historians' ultimate challenge is attempting to bring stability to naval history.

One major answer to this challenge is using vessels. However, just a minute fraction of the war vessels in famous engagements survive by means of preservation efforts. Even then, we see with the evolution of preserving ships as memorials some central questions arise: What are these for? To be preserved intact just like they appeared on the day of battle? To be morphed into a war memorial to remember the famous engagement and those sailors lost or to be transformed into an exhibition space for telling a greater story of a battle or nation?

This work will examine the inventive forms of memorial placement, including a national memorial in a nation's capital, modifying a decommissioned vessel into a memorial via exhibition, and memorialization of individual service personnel in their place of birth. These resourceful examples, among others, will demonstrate the imaginative nature of passing meaning of feats at sea on to a stationary location. Human invention can transcend the ever-changing ocean and bring some permanence to events that slowly recede into the past.

Reincarnation

One reoccurring theme throughout naval history is the reincarnation of ships' hulls. Whether from the Spanish Armada or the Japanese Navy in World War II, the conversion of a hull into another type of military or merchant vessel is ubiquitous. Forged from steel, welded or riveted, or carved from wood, these hulls possess incredible amounts of manpower and energy. Thus, in times of crisis, hulls quickly morph into new vessels, each with new crews, technologies, and names. In researching and designing museum products, one must be aware of the possibility of a single hull experiencing multiple reincarnations. Viewing this as a benefit as opposed to a chore grants the possibility of telling a multigenerational narrative with the use of a single hull.

A quick example is the first escort carrier of the U.S. Navy, the USS *Long Island*, CVE 1, which served as a small carrier in a host of auxiliary roles. First, in 1939, the hull was laid down as a merchant vessel to be christened the *Mormacmail*. Transferred to the U.S. Navy, in 1941, after conversion into a carrier, it sailed throughout World War II as the USS *Long Island*. After the war it was converted into a passenger ship the *Nelly* and shuttled war-ravaged immigrants fleeing Europe for Canada. Then, in 1953, morphing into the *Seven Seas*, she cruised the world's oceans as a floating university for college students. Lastly, in 1969, moored near the University of Rotterdam, the hull's final role included functioning as a floating dormitory until scrappage in the late 1970s.[12] In a single vessel, we see the human endeavors of commerce, warfare, and the pursuit of knowledge, and thus a single hull offers a wide window for naval interpretation.

Nomenclature

The issue of nomenclature is a huge factor in naval history effecting the naming of individual ships, entire classifications of vessels, and aspect of daily life aboard ship. Of the latter for example, stairs morph into "ladders," underwear is called "skivvy," and a bathroom is referred to as the "head." While the listing is extensive, for this work one point needs addressing: the connection of feminine terminology associated with talking about watercraft. This work will embrace the ancient maritime custom of referring to vessels as "her" or "she." Transcending languages and centuries, the origin of this practice has been lost and replaced with a plethora of speculative assertions. However, in thinking of the experience of those at sea since antiquity, it does not take a huge leap of imagination to draw connections to the lack of women at sea. This certainly could have germinated this tradition either in reference to the lack of female companionship at sea or the motherly love of a central vessel protecting sailors from the harsh ocean. While it is the choice of this author to use this nomenclature, it is completely up to the individual museum practitioner as to the usefulness or the appropriateness of using it. In either instance, however, it is important to understand that the use of "her" and "she," or other feminine terms, is pervasive in naval literature.

Best Practices

In a brief overview of best practices we will use a single institution devoted to preserving naval history to help us explore sound methodologies. A stellar organizational example is the Intrepid Sea, Air, and Space Museum Complex in New York City. Located on Pier 86 on the Hudson River on the west side of Manhattan, this ship-based organization demonstrates a number of best practices applicable to all naval interpretation.

Thus, let's start with their mission statement: "The mission of the Intrepid Sea, Air & Space Museum is to promote the awareness and understanding of history, science and service through its collections, exhibitions and programing in order to honor our heroes, educate the public and inspire our youth."[13]

While the scale of operations is massive, as the proximity to New York offers unprecedented funding and resource opportunities, the diverse operations completed by this organization provide helpful interpretive methods for organizations both large and small. Visitors can walk a flight deck full of historic aircraft or take a ride on a flight elevator designed to lift aircraft from the hangar to the flight deck. During warm summer evenings, visitors bring blankets and watch movies from the flight deck, including *Top Gun*, which is shown annually during the U.S. Navy's Fleet Week in late May. Creative use of exhibition space includes walking under a Space Shuttle orbiter and viewing an exhibit on the Hubble space telescope. Families can dine either in the galleys originally designed for the *Intrepid* crew, or on Pier 86 in the shade under the British Airways Concorde, the first and only turbojet supersonic airliner. All are examples of innovation that museum professionals can consider in revamping approaches to interpretation no matter their size or stated mission.

The Platform

Commissioned in August of 1943, the USS *Intrepid*, CV 11, served as an aircraft carrier until 1974. During World War II, she survived torpedo and kamikaze attacks. With three deployments in Southeast Asia during the Vietnam War, she experienced both differing generations of sailors and technology.[14] Today she rests as a memorial to the accomplishments of her sailors. While the museum today completes a host of historical functions, it all started with the preservation of the ship. With the help of their dedicated staff, the carrier's hull held up against Hurricane Sandy in 2013, thus protecting all it housed inside, including collection, archives, administrative space, and the newly arrived Space Shuttle orbiter *Enterprise* located on the aft portion of the flight deck.

Figure 1.2. Platform of war morphed into a platform of memory, the Intrepid Sea, Air, and Space Museum on the Hudson River in New York City. Photo by Jared Fiorato.

Figure 1.3. A 1/40th scale model of the *Intrepid* constructed of Legos gives a unique sense of scale as the 250,000 pieces composing the model weighs over five hundred pounds. Photo by Jared Fiorato.

Inclusive Collections

With an expansive mission, stretching beyond just the thirty-year era of Navy aviation on the résumé of CV 11, the organization successfully interprets a very inclusive definition of air and space history. Simply walking the museum's flight deck, visitors see a range of aircraft with no affiliation to naval aviation, such as the U.S. Air Force's SR-71 Blackbird designed for high-altitude reconnaissance and Soviet-designed Mig fighters. Inclusive collections, stemming from a carefully crafted and implemented mission statement, allow innovative accessioning practices and thus exhibitions. Looking beyond just interpreting one specific aircraft carrier and embracing a greater history of flight has produced organizational success.

Public Programs

Public programs introduce historical sites to new visitors for the first time. Partnering with outside organizations in hosting an event expands a circle of contacts for that given organization. While naval museums may first think of military topics as the only means to public programs, this is not the only game in town. A cornerstone of public programs on board the *Intrepid* is a place for remembrance for naval veterans from a range of ships and different eras of service; however, the organization has pushed beyond this one-dimensional form of engaging the public.

Teaming up with the Department of Homeless Services and the Administration of Children's Services, the educational department of the *Intrepid* designs special events for underserved children in the New York City area. Dr. Lynda Kennedy, the museum's vice president of education, in talking of the goal of such programs speaks to all museum professionals on our role in today's society. She said, "The exposure to the inspiration and wonder you find in this Museum can broaden a child's perspective and change her life."[15]

One particular program devoted to families and children with autism deserves attention. Realizing that one major barrier for kids with autism experiencing museums is the overload of sensory input, the education department and consultants developed a program that remained true to the museum's design while making it sensory sensitivity conscious. As one employee said, "A museum at full throttle is not sensory friendly."[16] With up to ten thousand visitors a day, a special program developed before normal hours allows families to engage exhibitions without the crowds. From the outside perspective, the museum would seen dimly lit and quiet, however, other aspects would appear like a regular day with kids landing paper airplanes on a simulated flight deck. In short, one regular attendee sums up the program with "Early Morning Operations has been such a liberating and enriching program for my family. I say 'liberating' because my children are free to experience the Museum's exhibits in ways that are more natural to them."[17]

Suggestions for Better Interpretation

To underscore the best practices considered throughout this work, after a number of case studies, bullets points will be listed. These small sections will reinforce the best practices used in the preceding case study. The overall goal of such areas is not disruption of the narrative, but rather highlighting the tactics that garnered successes in achieving the interpretative goals. Some case studies will not be followed by such sections, and it needs to be reinforced that case studies without bullet points are by no means lacking. However, due to the layout of the narrative, certain sections were selected to emphasize certain points, such as "inclusive use of objects used in an exhibition," as opposed to preceding and following examples.

Not Happy History

Finally, this work will include the use of collective memory in addressing the issue of mourning for individuals whose bodies were lost at sea. We will analyze not only how victims of sinkings dealt with the problematic issue of commemorating their lost ship, but also with the deaths of their fellow crewmembers. The Australian public historian Beth Gibbings addresses the issue of commemoration of those lost at sea and focuses on the loss of the vessel the *SIEV X* while attempting to reach Australia with fleeing refugees. Her work sets the theoretical stage for memorialization and mourning at sea. She writes, "This story deals particularly with the question of how deaths can be remembered and mourned without bodies after a tragedy at sea."[18] Furthermore, Gibbings argues that closure could be reached through imaginative means; the lack of the victims' bodies can be transcended. She writes, "The absence of bodies has not stood in the way of commemoration, but the status of the lives that were lost—both personally and symbolically—has been important in shaping the memorials."[19] With regard to veterans, for those who survive the loss of a ship, the call to memorialize their deceased comrades in arms and bring closure is just as important as with any other tragedy. This work will explore the collective memory of those who experienced loss on the seas inventing ways of filling the emotional void of not holding a funeral in a traditional sense.

What Is at Stake?

In short, if entities devoted to public memory fail in their stated mission, some other entity can step in and fill the void, and not always with the best of intentions in mind. Failing to meet our obligations, we leave naval topics vulnerable to the for-profit model, and thus respectfully remembering the victims lost in any naval tragedy is threatened. Especially for naval disasters such as the *Titanic*, a recent for-profit model demonstrates both the lack of respect for those who survived and flirts with flippancy toward those who perished. A simple visit to this for-profit corporation's website demonstrates this concept. The "Titanic: World's Largest Museum Attraction" has two locations, one in Branson, Missouri, and the other in Pigeon Forge, Tennessee. At the risk of sounding arrogant and elitist, names and titles matter. Are we comfortable with the word *attraction* attached to a museum disseminating information on the deaths of some 1,500 people? Or an online gift shop selling the "exclusive" Titanic perfume at $40 a bottle without mentioning those lost, such as the fifty-three children that perished?[20]

While this author has not visited either site, the promotional website alone sets the tone of this for-profit entity interpreting history. With a key demographic of young visitors, tea times for kids are scheduled to learn of the grandeur of the vessel, along with touching an iceberg. The very top of the homepage speaks volumes, with Titanic Vacation Packages offering discounts on packaged visits to The Comedy Bark Theater, Dolly Parton's Dixie Stampede, and Silver Dollar City.

Profit is not a dirty word. Financial solvency is a key issue for all long-term successful nonprofits devoted to preserving and protecting history, especially so for smaller organizations. However, the tactic of near erasure of victims to sell an experience is what we are up against. This disrespects not only those victims who were lost and survived, but also the intelligence of visitors. To use our frame of reference, could we imagine an "attraction" in eighty years' time based on the last few hours of the Windows of the World Restaurant on the top of the North Tower of the World Trade Center? These for-profit models we see in Missouri and Tennessee, of claiming a tragedy on the high seas in the name of profit, should be a warning cry for all public historians on naval topics.

Notes

1. Rainer F. Buschmann, *Oceans in World History* (Boston: McGraw Hill Higher Education, 2007), 2.

2. Bernhard Klein and Gesa Mankenthum, eds., *Sea Changes: Historicizing the Ocean* (New York: Routledge, 2004), 2.

3. Pierre Nora, "Between Memory and History: Les Lieux de Memoire," *Representations* no. 26 (1989): 8.

4. Ibid., 9.

5. Ibid., 8.

6. Ibid., 23.

7. Ibid., 22.

8. "Acquisitions & Accessioning," University of Alaska Museum of the North, https://www.uaf.edu/museum/collections/ethno/policies/acquisitions/ (accessed August 25, 2015).

9. "Aircraft & Exhibits," National Naval Aviation Museum, http://www.navalaviationmuseum.org/attractions/aircraft-exhibits/ (accessed August 25, 2015).

10. "Nautical Nights Overnight Program," Battleship Cove Celebrating 50 Years, http://www.battleshipcove.org/nautical-nights/ (accessed August 27, 2015).

11. James D. Hornfischer, *The Last Stand of the Tin Can Sailors: The Extraordinary World War II Story of the U.S. Navy's Finest Hour* (New York: Random House, 2004), 359.

12. "Long Island II (CVE-1)," Naval History and Heritage Command, http://www.history.navy.mil/research/histories/ship-histories/danfs/l/long-island-ii.html (accessed August 12, 2015).

13. "Where Information Meets Wonder," Intrepid Sea, Air, and Space Museum Highlights Report, Fiscal years 2013 and 2014, 2.

14. "USS Intrepid (CV 11)," Naval History and Heritage Command, http://www.history.navy.mil/our-collections/photography/us-navy-ships/aircraft-carriers/uss-intrepid--cv-11-.html (accessed August 21, 2015).

15. "Where Information Meets Wonder," Intrepid Sea, Air, and Space Museum Highlights Report, Fiscal years 2013 and 2014, 12.

16. Ibid.

17. Ibid., 13.

18. Beth Gibbings, "Remembering the SIEV X: Who Care for the Bodies of the Stateless, Lost at Sea?" *The Public Historian* 32, no. 1 (2010): 15.

19. Ibid.

20. "Titanic Merchandise-Featured Items," Titanic: World's Largest Museum Attraction, https://www.titanicpigeonforge.com/cart_display.php?c=featured (accessed August 19, 2015).

CHAPTER 2

Commemoration

FOR THIS CHAPTER, we are interested in the use of the symbolic meaning of any aspect of naval history. Entities such as individuals and cities can use symbolic meaning to make connections to such concepts as wartime victory, communal loss, or shared national experience. The commemoration process must undergo a negotiation of sorts in determining how, what, and who is commemorated. The possible results include civic markers, memorial services, exhibitions in museums, or items on display at a local veteran's organization. As for naval topics specifically for this study, we are interested in the differing processes that occur in attempting to bridge the factor of the ocean. Unlike land battles, which later can serve as a stationary platform, the remaining debris from naval battles sinks, departs, or drifts away. With no earth to service as a foundation for memorial or graves, man's need to find closure and meaning with naval commemoration transcends this gap with the help of invention. This inventive nature in commemoration of actions on the high seas can be seen in Oklahoma.

A Submarine in Oklahoma

If you are traveling across eastern Oklahoma on Interstate 40, posted road signs list the turn-off for Muskogee. For most, this brings to mind the Merle Haggard song released in 1969 confronting the radical student movement of the Vietnam-era "Okie From Muskogee" with such classic lines as "We still wave Old Glory down at the courthouse" and "A place where even squares can have a ball."[1] However, other signs designate a municipal park, which is rather stunning to the viewer's eyes. At the Muskogee War Memorial Park is the USS *Batfish*, a World War II–era U.S. Navy submarine.

The USS *Batfish*, SS 310, in her seven cruises in World War II is credited with sinking thirteen Japanese vessels, including three submarines. During her patrols, she launched over seventy torpedoes, eradicating over thirty-five thousand tons of enemy shipping. Named after a species of West Indian fish, she is one of the most successful submarines in history. World War II was the glory days of the U.S. Navy submarine service as they helped break the back of the Japanese economy by destroying their merchant marine fleet, and thus the empires ability to transport. However, the costs were high, as fifty-two American submarines and some 3,500 sailors perished in the conflict. The term *Eternal Patrol* surfaced after the war, marking the lost vessels and sailors of the submarine service. In 1956, the United States Submarine Veterans of World War II incorporated as a national organization, with chapters located in individual states and the goal of perpetuating the heritage of the submarine service, which included the use of decommissioned vessels in acts of commemoration.

Transforming decommissioned submarines into memorials or museums first took place on the coasts. However, in the late 1960s and early 1970s, some asked the question, "Why not a submarine in Oklahoma?" While outside the scope of this study, this Oklahoma-based effort would provide a compelling case study in public/private partnerships, river transport logistics, and volunteers not giving up on an idea. Today the *Batfish* serves as the centerpiece at the Muskogee War Memorial Park in commemorating all Oklahoma veterans from all wars and from all branches of the U.S. military.

The park opened in 1973. Located on eight acres along the riverfront of the Arkansas River, the *Batfish* is on display inset in concrete and next to a 2,500 square foot military museum. On the *Batfish* adults and children tour the cramped quarters, see the tiny cooking spaces, and imagine life on board for weeks, if not months, at a time. Landscaping and picnic areas of the memorial park include other weapons transformed into commemorative artifacts that include a World War I field cannon, torpedoes from World War II, and a Vietnam-era self-propelled howitzer. In 2010, the park acquired a unique piece that connects Oklahoma with the U.S. Navy, this being a piece of the battleship USS *Oklahoma*, BB 37.

Sunk in the shallow waters of Pearl Harbor in December of 1941, the battleship was later deemed only worthy of scrap. However, in 1946 she was lost in transit in a Pacific storm en route to the scrapyards in San Francisco. The following year the U.S. Navy in a dredging operation located a piece of the fire control mast from BB 37 on the bottom of Pearl Harbor. Thanks to the same preservation efforts that saved the *Batfish*, the U.S. Navy agreed to loan this last portion of the battleship *Oklahoma* to the memorial park.

The use of SS 310 as a focal point for commemorating Oklahoma's larger connections to U.S. military history is diverse and multifaceted. The Muskogee War Memorial Park holds exhibitions and events such as "Invasion Yanqui: The U.S. Mexican War," *Batfish* living history day, and an exhibition on objects left as personal memorials at the Murrah Federal Building on the site of the 1995 bombing in Oklahoma City. But an event that occurs every May is the most unique in terms of commemorating naval history. Called the "Tolling of the Boats," this event utilizes the *Batfish* and the memorial space surrounding it in commemorating the fifty-two U.S. submarines lost in World War II. Teaming up with the United States Submarine

Veterans of World War II, it is the central commemorative event of the annual *Batfish* reunion. During the ceremony, the name of each submarine lost in the war is read aloud, followed by the tolling the *Batfish*'s bell marking the loss of the individual submarines and their crews on the Enteral Patrol.[2] Indeed, commemorating naval history in Muskogee, Oklahoma, with a World War II–era submarine has granted the community a portal of remembering, and thus interpreting, a larger portion of the military history of the United States.

Best Practices and Suggestions for Better Interpretation

- Inclusive approach to interpretation in embracing the history of all U.S. Navy submarines at one site.
- Commemoration activities at site allow for public events to honor all American veterans, not just those of the U.S. Navy or World War II.
- Superb example of a volunteer effort composed of original thinkers and a driving enthusiasm in getting a unique idea off the ground—that of a submarine memorial in Oklahoma.

Myth Making

Public historians must understand the formation and role of myths and the potential minefield for those who challenge such myths. The process of constructing an overarching tale, or myth, is a story as old as mankind. The French philosopher and historian Mircea Eliade, in his work *The Myth of the Eternal Return*, investigates the construction of myths in what he terms "archaic" societies. He argues that early societies faced difficulty in holding on to specific facts, like actual names and events, for more than a few centuries. Faced with the inability to remember specific events and individuals, these societies utilized myths. As he writes, "The historical personage is assimilated to his mythical model (hero, etc.), while the event is identified with the category of mythical actions (fight with a monster, enemy brothers, etc.)."[3] Eliade theorizes that myths function as a means of making sense of events that normally face oblivion as a result of a society forgetting all the specific details over time. He suggests that while the construction of myth marginalizes many specific details on a particular topic, the myth functions in streamlining the narrative and thus preserving the overarching importance of the actual events. This foundational understanding of the role of myth, or the invention of narrative to allow smoother transfer of central themes by disregarding most of the specific details, is much older than our profession as historians. Thus, disregarding numerous specific details in the forming of a commemorative product is not only allowed, but with the complexity of the modern warfare, is also required for a coherent product.

The historian Joseph Amato, in his work *Guilt and Gratitude: A Study of the Origins of Contemporary Conscience*, traces humanity's relationship with a number of governing authorities, including tribal groups and religious states. Amato theorizes that central to any society's order is the group's collective experience, which for nearly all groups embraces the passing on of tales and myths. The purpose of such myths is to deliver meaning to individuals who did not experience the story firsthand, either as the result of geography or time. With the rise of nation-states, however, Amato asserts that a shift takes place for these new citizens. He writes, "Events, therefore, for contemporary man are the landmarks of his existence."[4] As nation-states expanded in size and influence, the very events, which form the basis of the identity of citizens, may be experienced by only a handful of citizens. Amato argues that while the practice is not new, the scale imposed by the nation-state in myth making greatly transforms the construction of the myth. As Amato writes, "To a large degree, national societies exist by virtue of having a mentality formed out of events experienced and valued collectively. In this manner, the citizens of a nation continue to live the experiences of the past long after they have happened."[5] Thus, encapsulating naval myth into a national story necessitates the purging of most individual experiences and memories.

Pearl Harbor

U.S. naval history is so engrained in place names of the nation that over time these can lose the original nautical meaning. For example, twenty cities in the United States are named Decatur, after one of the first heroes of the U.S. Navy. Stephen Decatur Jr. rose to national fame in the now long forgotten Barbary Wars in which the young U.S. Navy battled warlords in North Africa engaged in piracy. However, how many residents of Decatur, Iowa, understand the namesake of their hometown?[6] Or even that the name has a connection to naval history?

On the other end of the spectrum, a handful of location names can be overshadowed by an event that took place there. When this occurs, it is also easy to forget decades later that the memorial marking this event developed over time. Memorialization took place, designers imagined, and finally decisions were made about the commemoration. As we have seen in lower Manhattan with the World Trade Center site, in the wake of the attacks of 9/11 almost immediately ideas were publicly floated on what to do with the site to commemorate the victims.

Complexity of events seeks simplified reductions. This does not mean that people seek simple answers, but that with modernity there is just too much stimulus at times. As with Pearl Harbor, in seeking one symbol of the attack of December 1941 a plethora of possibilities lay smoldering in the ruins. However, with of all the stricken down vessels, planes, and individual servicemen, over time meaning coalesced around one vessel, the USS *Arizona*, BB 39. A single Japanese bomb, which penetrated the forward magazine, caused a horrific explosion that sank the over thirty-thousand-ton vessel in under ten minutes. In the shallow harbor, the ocean waters consumed the hull; however, her superstructure remained surfaced.[7] The billowing black smoke from the charred steel wreckage, with 1,177 sailors entombed inside, granted photographers a powerful image in symbolizing American defeat. On a Sunday in December the words "Pearl Harbor" transformed from a geographic location into a term conveying a range of emotions including loss, hate, and bewilderment.

In terms of commemoration, the memorial to BB 39 has come to symbolize much more than just one vessel. As the site of the single largest loss of life, she and the sailors entombed inside over the decades have morphed into the specific place to commemorate the entire attack on Hawaii that included Ford Island and numerous other military installations on the island of Oahu. Visitors to the memorial atop BB 39 look down on the wreck and still see trace amounts of oil bubbling up from the submerged capital ship. In a way, this is a fitting ceremonial act, reminding twenty-first-century visitors of her former life, that of a proud ship of war. She too, like the sailors inside on that Sunday morning, had her life ahead of her before a surprise attack cut all of these lives violently short.

On the national level, the Alfred Preis–designed memorial dedicated in 1962 that rests on the sunken hull of BB 39 encapsulates American remembrance of the attack. All memorialization is a process of negotiation, so too with the sunken hull of BB 39. In 1943, concepts surfaced for a memorial. Six years later, the Territory of Hawaii formed the Pacific War Memorial Commission. However, the project gained a huge ally in 1958 with President Dwight D. Eisenhower approving a national memorial. On December 7, 1958, the popular television show "This Is Your Life" raised $94,000 in viewer donations, and in 1961, the young Elvis Presley hosted a benefit concert gathering funds for the memorial. After a four-year process, the memorial, a 184-foot-long white open-air structure that rests on the midsection of the submerged hull, was dedicated to all military personnel that died in the attack. For the structure itself, the designer wrote, "Wherein the structure sags in the center but stands strong and vigorous at the ends, expresses initial defeat and ultimate victory. . . . The overall effect is one of serenity."[8]

The design structure has three main sections, composed of an entry room, assembly area, and shrine to those that perished. The main logistical challenge for managing the site is visitors needing to arrive by boat, as it rests above the sunken battleship, and thus the need for the entry room for visitors preparing to arrive and leave the memorial. The assembly area allows for the gathering of public ceremonies in a central area. Lastly and most important in terms of commemoration, is the shrine room that lists in etched marble the names of those killed on the *Arizona*. In black letters standing out against the white marble, names are listed in alphabetical order. Set in the middle of the names is the following: "To The Memory of the Gallant Men Here Entombed and Their Shipmates Who Gave Their Lives In Action On December 7, 1941 on the U.S.S. Arizona."[9]

As addressed in chapter 1, public historians commemorating with naval topics are at a disadvantage with battles normally taking place on the open sea and thus lacking a land-based location for memorial placement. However, this is not necessarily true with a handful of battles taking place near a shoreline, or more specifically in a harbor. As the attack on Pearl Harbor shows, commemoration of a battle on the sea is possible on site with large numbers of visitors if a suitable nearby land location grants open access. However, we would be mistaken to think that this attack is only remembered in Hawaii as a strong link to the attack on Pearl Harbor is seen in Arizona, a state known for its deserts and mountain ranges and without a single mile of coastline.

Whereas the wreckage of BB 39 came to symbolize all the events of December 7, 1941, in Hawaii, for the state of Arizona, the battleship's meaning materialized in a different manor. The first official state-level memorial to the fallen vessel took place in the year full of Americans' searching for meaning, the national Bicentennial. In 1976, the nation searched for a solid foundation after ten years of upheaval with race riots, the Vietnam War, and Watergate. A group of Arizona citizens and organizations lobbied successfully with the U.S. Navy for a permanent loan, that of a nineteen-thousand-pound anchor salvaged from the wreck of BB 39. Forged in Chester, Pennsylvania, in 1911, the anchor with serial number A-277 stands fourteen feet tall and for twenty years served on board the USS *Arizona*.[10] Thirty-five years after Pearl Harbor, citizens of the state of Arizona sought to morph this anchor into a memorial.

Resting on top of a circular cement platform on the lawn to the east of the Arizona State Capitol dome, the anchor-turned-memorial stands near one of the masts also recovered from BB 39. Bronze plaques around the circumference of the cement base list the names of all the sailors stationed on the ill-fated battleship who did not survive. However, while the national memorial to BB 39 symbolizes the entire attack on Pearl Harbor, in dedicating this memorial, Governor Raul Castro clearly noted the importance of this anchor to the residents of Arizona. On the sunny December day, he stated to the gathered crowd, "The anchor is a symbol, a fitting memorial for a ship that will never again sail. A reminder of the solid substance and lasting merit of our nation and the people who have served in our armed forces."[11] While for the nation the demise of the USS *Arizona* encapsulated December 7, for Arizona thirty-five years after the attack this piece of BB 39 encompassed a memorial for American veterans of all wars. Although the divergence may seem subtle, for pubic historians it is critical to realize the difference. At a time when the wounds of Vietnam were still raw, with no real national discussion of a memorial to Vietnam veterans, Governor Castro took the ecumenical approach in the dedication to encompass all veterans. Going beyond BB 39, or even all World War II veterans, Castro expanded the symbolic meaning of the nineteen-thousand-pound anchor.

The state of Arizona's commemoration of Pearl Harbor did not end with the Bicentennial. The State Capitol Museum, located in the Capitol building, served as a depositary and archive for BB 39 material culture and also produced a permanent exhibition on the battleship titled "U.S.S. Arizona: Flagship of the Fleet." Showcasing the images and objects, such as silverware, from BB 39, the permanent exhibition highlights the long working career of the vessel beyond just her last violent ten minutes from the time she was struck and quickly sank.[12]

Best Practices and Suggestions for Better Interpretation

- These Arizona examples clearly demonstrate that naval history is not a monopoly of seaside communities.
- Demonstrate that the loss of a ship at sea can be overcome, either with the placement of a memorial on top of the sunken BB 39 or with objects from the vessel such as the anchor.
- Shows the symbolic power that artifacts retain in naval commemoration.

Figure 2.1. One of the anchors of the USS *Arizona*, BB 39, in front of the Arizona State Capitol in Phoenix, was dedicated as a marker to all American veterans. Photo by Ben Hruska.

Japan

Yamato

The largest battleship ever constructed, *Yamato* was just one of two such vessels completed during World War II by the Empire of Japan. Displacing 70,000 tons, a crew of 2,750 sailors, and 863 feet in length, she literally dwarfed all battleships from the First World War era. One hundred and fifty thousand shaft horsepower moved her bulk at twenty-seven knots. Her three sets of large naval guns included 200mm, 410mm, and the main turrets of 650mm. She was a tribute to the rapid modernization of Japanese military, society, and culture that in just under a century threw off its centuries-long isolationist practices that shunned Western influences. In 1853, after American commodore Matthew Perry landed and opened Japan when it was forced to sign a treaty permitting trade with the United States, Western influences poured in. Ninety years later, the empire launched the *Yamato* on December 16, 1941. Only one problem: nine days before this was the surprise attack on Pearl Harbor, which today historians agree is the very moment when naval strategy shifted away from the concept of the battleship.

In April 1945, tracked by U.S. submarines and carrier aircraft and sustaining hours of bombing and torpedo attacks, the *Yamato* sank from internal explosions and only 269 sailors survived.[13] While whatever remains of her is on the Pacific's bottom north of Okinawa, Japan today commemorates the *Yamato* at a museum in Kure, Japan. Located on the waterfront where she was built, she is not commemorated as a weapon of war but rather has been reframed as an example of Japanese science and technology.

The Yamato Kure Maritime Museum is located just a short train ride from downtown Hiroshima. Rather than focusing on the battleship as a weapon of war and commemorating the Japanese naval actions in World War II, the site attempts to remember the connection of the harbor city of Kure and the technological achievement in the construction of the largest battleship. As stated on the opening screen of the website, "We wish to convey the history of 'Kure' which made the Battleship *Yamato*, importance of peace and the splendor of science and technology to the future."[14] Upon entering the four-floor museum is a 1/10th scale model of the battleship *Yamato*. The immaculately detailed model, over eighty feet in length, attracts visitors young and old alike. However, framing the battleship as a link to a nation's technological accomplishments rather than military heritage and strength offers a unique case study in naval interpretation.

The introductory text on the museum contains just one sentence on World War II, which contrasts sharply with commemoration of naval museums in Britain, the United States, and Australia. It states, "Once Kure flourished as the greatest naval port in the East, as well as the greatest naval arsenal in Japan, which built the most powerful battleship YAMATO."[15] The commemorative focus is the technology used in constructing such vessels, which when applied to peaceful purposes in the postwar period to tanker and freighter construction transformed Japan into the largest shipbuilding economy in the world by 1960. This naval narrative is not just a story of Kure rising from the ashes of war, but also of the modernization of Japan embracing the concept of a Westernized democratic capitalism. As it states, "'Yamato Museum' introduces the 'History of Kure' and a broad range of 'Science and Technologies' including shipbuilding and steelmaking which have served as a foundation for the modernization of Japan, with a perspective on the efforts of our predecessors and lifestyles and cultures of that time."[16]

Other weapons on display, such as the Mitsubishi Zero fighter aircraft and the Kalten Human Torpedo Type 10, are all viewed through the lens of the technology required in the production rather than militarist expansion by Japan. Ignored is the concept of such weapons utilized by indoctrinated fanatics in suicide missions. Additionally, with the use of hands-on learning exhibitions, the third floor is devoted to shipbuilding technology stemming from the *Yamato*. The fourth floor observation terrace allows for a commanding panoramic view of where the *Yamato* was constructed and the modern-day shipbuilding facilities of Kure, from which visitors can see down to what is the most imaginative aspect of commemorating the battleship.

Stretching away from the museum is a nearly one-thousand-foot-long pier that grants the visitor a sense of scale. Jetting into the busy Kure harbor, the pier is inset with design features that hint at the true size of the *Yamato*. On its center is a walled-off area with metal railings designating the battleship superstructure, while round designs walked over by visitors mark the location of her guns. Commemorating technology and design, rather than war, is seen in the linear center of the wharf with green space with abundant flowers, shrubs, and trees. Display panels also bring context into *Yamato*'s scale, and again text focuses on the construction of such a vessel rather than its intended mission. Lastly, other visitors walking around the pier add an additional sense of scale.[17]

Naval technology designed for warfare transformed into peaceful maritime construction in the postwar period is commemorated on the waterfront of Kure. Interpreting a World War II–era weapon from the perspective of technology and innovation might be the only method for Japan in commemorating a time period full of atrocities committed throughout Asia against civilians, most notably in China and Korea. That being said, framing the *Yamato* as a window into human ingenuity of technology, which after the war assisted in rebuilding Japan into postwar prosperity, is nothing short of brilliant. This almost singular focus on technology is truly a unique example of interpreting naval history.

Best Practices and Suggestions for Better Interpretation

- Inventive interpretation: not centering on the *Yamato* as a window for commemorating war, but instead of exploring science and technology.
- Prime example of commemoration with models: an eighty-foot model welcomes visitors and grounds their experience for the exhibitions and public spaces that await them.

Mikasa

However, Japan does in fact commemorate a ship of war in the more traditional sense, by using a former war vessel as means of celebrating a military victory that occurred in the very first part of the twentieth century. The battleship HIJMS *Mikasa* served as the flagship of the Japanese Navy's stunning victory over a European foe in 1905, thus making a bold statement to the Western world of a power shift commencing in the Pacific. The defeated Russian Navy at the Battle of Tsushima Strait lost almost its entire fleet and suffered 4,500 dead and 6,100 captured sailors. The dramatic end of the Russo-Japanese War claimed only 116 dead Japanese sailors. While *Mikasa* led the Japanese Navy to victory, peace was not so kind, as in the years following the war a massive internal explosion in the magazine compartment sank her. Despite a great loss of life, she was repaired and placed in the reserve fleet.

At the close of World War I, the Washington Naval Conference of 1922 produced an arms control treaty and signing nations reduced their floating tonnage of war vessels. The treaty relegated the *Mikasa* to the scrapyard; however, Japan applied for a special exemption in an effort to save her as a platform of commemorating the 1905 Japanese victory. In 1924, the HIJMS *Mikasa* Preservation Society formed and successfully completed the required stipulations of the agreed-upon exemption. Set in concert fixing her position in Yokohama harbor, the four-hundred-foot battleship points toward the Imperial Palace in Tokyo and the surrounding land near her was transformed into a public park commemorating the successful war against the Russian Empire.

The history of the *Mikasa* as a commemorative space is ironic in that she survived World War II relatively unscathed but suffered greatly in the immediate postwar peace. During the American occupation after the war, she was deemed a threat, and the bridge, guns, and masts were removed from the fifty-year-old battleship. But by the mid-1950s, the perceived militaristic threat of the immediate postwar period vanished, and with the support of U.S. Navy fleet commander Chester Nimitz, the Japanese government started the restoration of Memorial Ship *Mikasa*. Ceremonially rededicated on May 27, 1961, a fully restored battleship reopened marking the Japanese victory at the Battle of Tsushima Strait.[18] Today this public space that merges a green space and a battleship-turned-museum stands as a unique form of commemoration of two empires, that of the victorious Japanese over the Russian. While neither exist today as political entities, the actions of these empires echo well into twenty-first-century geopolitics.

U.S. Postal Service

An example of the various ways of commemorating the attack on Pearl Harbor occurred in 1991 with the fiftieth anniversary. The U.S. Postal Service issued a stamp of an artist's rendition of the attack with numerous battleships on fire billowing black smoke. This stamp, however, was just one in a long line of commemorative stamps of military subjects. With regard to naval history, stamps have marked the service of admirals and sailors, fleets and individual vessels, and events from the American Revolution into the post–Cold War period.

Commemoration via stamps has a long history. In fact, the first two stamps issued by the U.S. Post Office in 1847 marked the careers of two Founding Fathers with strong military connections. George Washington of course was the first president and also led the Continental Army, and Benjamin Franklin, in his younger days, served in the Pennsylvania militia. Stamps serve as a means of communicating in two ways. First, stamps allow the movement of pieces of mail around the country. Second, stamps themselves serve as a small canvas for any issuing nation, and thus a perfect platform for commemoration.

The 1990s ushered in stamps commemorating naval aspects of the war with the fiftieth anniversaries of key events in World War II. In 1991, a stamp was issued marking the Liberty Ships, which proved amazingly important in moving vast amounts of men and material during the war. The following year, the Battle of Midway was commemorated with a stamp showing the wounded aircraft carrier the USS *Yorktown*. However, this stamp series from the 1990s was just one link in the chain of a long history of naval commemoration. In 1937, the USPS issued a stamp recognizing the U.S. Naval Academy, and, in 1961, issued a stamp marking the heritage of naval aviation. One of the most striking stamps in terms of artwork, issued in 1945, commemorated the entire U.S. Navy. Using blue ink combined with a white background, the stamp portrays a group of anonymous smiling young sailors with their white caps on.

Figure 2.2. The United States Postal Service has a long history of commemorating aspects of American naval history. Photo by Ben Hruska.

Best Practices and Suggestions for Better Interpretation

- Showcases how national identity can be shaped by naval actions at sea.
- Demonstrates an air museum based on historic aircraft embracing other forms of commemoration, including a nation commemorating aircraft with the issuing of a series of stamps.

After 1995 and the ending of the fiftieth anniversaries of World War II series, the USPS was not finished honoring naval history. A series titled "Classic American Aircraft" highlighted our nation's aviation history, and one such stamp was of the Vought F4C Corsair. The Corsair, a gulf-winged fighter, is one of the most famed aircraft of World War II and saw active naval service into the 1960s.[19] The commemorative means of this stamp is expressed in a brilliant method at the Pima Air Museum in Tucson, Arizona. In a section of the main hangar devoted to naval aviation, where aircraft such as an F-14 Tomcat and a TMF Avenger are displayed, a large blowup of the Corsair stamp hangs suspended from the ceiling. The use of a USPS stamp is very effective and, more importantly, brings to life the fact that commemoration can exist in sizes both large and small.

Silver Screen

Commemoration can take place on the silver screen, and in fact Hollywood and the U.S. Navy even teamed up during wartime to produce films centered on remembering naval actions. One film produced during World War II stands out as a prime example of the U.S. Navy offering its support in the filming of a movie on an individual aircraft carrier. Like many movies about the war, *Thirty Seconds Over Tokyo* was initially a book. Written by Ted Lawson, who participated in the raid depicted, was a member of the U.S. Army Air Corp and his book grants a colorful account of Lieutenant Colonel James Doolittle's raid of B-25 Air Army Corp bombers improvising an attack on the Japanese homelands by launching these land-based aircraft from a U.S. Navy aircraft carrier.[20] The film, released in 1944, highlighted the action of volunteers who gave the United States a huge propaganda victory in bombing the mainland of Japan just months after Pearl Harbor.

The film stressed the military's lack of interservice rivalry with the U.S. Army Air Corp working in unison with the U.S. Navy. However, the movie reinforces the notion that one large aircraft carrier, the USS *Hornet*, CV 8, single-handedly launched the mission. No attention is paid to the other fifteen vessels involved in the operation. Only the men in the B-25s and the *Hornet* are highlighted.[21] The entire mission, involving thousands of service members and sixteen ships, was encapsulated to focus on the bomber crews and the *Hornet*'s flight deck. While this simplified screenplay allows the viewer to better digest a complicated secret mission, this comes at the expense of marginalizing the other vessels involved in the operation. Further adding to the film's impact for the wartime viewers was the censorship during the war, which suppressed many of the specific details about the operation until after the conflict. While an example of commemoration taking place during the war, this film perpetuated national narrative that remembered certain missions and certain ships and shunned the vast majority of wartime experiences.

Navy Day 1945

The U.S. Navy has a long history of self-commemorating, including Navy Day. This date took on exceedingly high importance at the close of World War II with nationwide events on Navy Day, October 27, 1945, organized by the U.S. Navy in order to present their branch of the service to the American public. A range of war vessels poured into the ports of San Francisco, New Orleans, and Baltimore, and in interior cities smaller navy vessels sailed up the Mississippi River to St. Louis and Dubuque, Iowa.[22] However, the major commemorative event was in New York City. An estimated one million people gathered in Central Park to hear a speech from President Harry Truman, forty-seven vessels were on display on the Hudson River, and 1,200 planes flew overhead in a single formation.[23] Before these grand events took place, however, a single ceremony kicked off the day's events: the dedication of a monument to the late president Franklin D. Roosevelt.

When President Truman's motorcade entered the Brooklyn Naval Yard, ten thousand people waited on the deck of the soon to be commissioned aircraft carrier. Those gathered included the new ship's band, the honor guard, and a group of sailors who carried out a two-hundred-pound cake. The cake was a replica of the ship, the newest in a series of aircraft carriers. President Truman would officially commission this new carrier as an act of commemoration to the deceased President Roosevelt.

In his speech dedicating the forty-five-thousand-ton carrier, the USS *Franklin D. Roosevelt*, CV 42, the president spoke in glowing terms of President Roosevelt's relationship with the U.S. Navy. He stated, "His name is engraved on this great carrier, as it is in the hearts of men and women of goodwill the world over—Franklin D. Roosevelt."[24] Truman stated that this new carrier symbolized "our commitment to the United Nations Organization to reach out anywhere in the world and to help peace-loving nations of the world stop any international gangster."[25] He closed his verbal tribute by speaking of the challenges facing America in the postwar era. He stated, "But we approach them in the spirit of Franklin D. Roosevelt whose words are inscribed in bronze on this vessel: 'We can, we will, we must!'"[26] The commissioning ceremony included 125 navy planes flying in formation spelling out three letters: FDR. In honoring the president who led the nation through the Great Depression and to victory in World War II, the monument selected within six months of his death commemorating his life was an aircraft carrier.

Bicentennial

The Bicentennial provided the United States with a platform for reorientation with its past. A vast range of events transpired during the celebration of America's two hundredth birthday: the Department of the Treasury issued Bicentennial coins, NASA officially debuted the Space Shuttle, and the Smithsonian opened the National Air and Space Museum. The historian John Bodnar wrote that the Bicentennial gave Americans a chance to move away from the divisive decade of the 1960s. He wrote, "For many Americans the weekend celebration surrounding July 4, 1976, marked an end to a period of social unrest and dissent and a renewal of American consensus and patriotism."[27] In addition, feature films gave millions of Americans a chance to experience aspects of the American past, which included revisiting the naval war in World War II.

World War II held a unique place in American memory because it did not represent division, but unity. The nostalgia surrounding World War II increased with the civic breakdown of the 1960s. As Philip Beidler wrote, "The glow of 1945 persists as a kind of beacon, a moment in which American's attitudes toward themselves and their relations to the world at least once seem to have been filled with a clarity and purpose."[28] In comparison with other aspects of the American past, such as slavery, Indian removal, and suppression of women's rights, World War II held the possibility to be framed in the light of a high collective moral task.

One topic that met all the goals of a clear moral delineation between good and evil, thus avoiding more complicated topics, was the Battle of Midway. The noted military historian John Keegan wrote about how the battle served as a wonderful topic for future myth making. He wrote, "Midway, the turning-point battle of the Pacific War, was a contest between American and Japanese maritime technology, expressed in numbers and quality of carriers and carrier aircraft deployed."[29] This epic tide-turning sea battle as a topic of celebration required an equally powerful medium for the American Bicentennial audience.

This feature film not only included the biggest vessels yet shown on film, but also the greatest and most dramatic Pacific victory. The film *Midway*, released in 1976, included a cast of major stars such as Charlton Heston, Glenn Ford, and Henry Fonda and depicted the carrier battle of World War II that turned the tide of the war in America's favor. However, even this cast of stars and a screenplay about a major sea victory was not big enough. The film also required the placement of special speakers in movie theaters because it utilized Sensurround, allowing for the segregation of sounds for the audience, thus highlighting the noises of individual crashes, explosions, and aircraft engines.

The producer of the film, Walter Mirisch, sought to develop a film about the Battle of Midway for the Bicentennial. The film presented a much easier story to tell the American audience in 1976 when compared with other aspects of the war such as the use of atomic weapons. Mirisch, realizing that he needed U.S. Navy assistance in the production of the film, sent a draft to the naval service in late 1974. A communiqué within the navy demonstrated their take on the possibilities of the film, as it stated, "[film] could be useful in recruiting efforts as part of the Bicentennial and as an adjunct to the Sea-Air Operations Hall of the new Air and Space Museum which will focus on carriers."[30] The navy thus offered the services of a World War II–era carrier, the USS *Lexington*, CV 16, and filming took place on board in the Gulf of Mexico, where the flight deck of the *Lexington* served as the decks of both American and Japanese carriers.[31]

The film's overall narrative focused on the power of carriers. The Japanese demonstrated the major shift in tactics with the ascent of the carrier over the battleship and its surprise carrier-based attack on Pearl Harbor. The film depicted the vulnerability of the U.S. Navy in early 1942. The theme of the film is that brave naval aviators and bold decisions by admirals brought about the destruction of four Japanese carriers.[32] With a major film commemorating the naval war of World War II, in a year celebrating the birth of the United States, the Battle of Midway was introduced to a new, younger American audience. When the noted military movie historian Lawrence Suid interviewed Mirisch about the meaning of the film released in 1976, he rejected the concept of trying to forget Vietnam and the turmoil of the 1960s. Suid wrote, for Mirisch, "*Midway* simply helped young people learn about World War II and the major turning point in the war against Japan."[33]

A reviewer in the *New York Times* praised the film for bringing this story of World War II to modern viewers. It stated, "It was the turning point of the war against the Japanese who lost four carriers and never again seriously threatened American sea power in the central Pacific."[34] The reviewer was critical of some portions of the film, including certain adaptations in the script, and he urged those interested in a more accurate account to read the works of the renowned naval scholar Samuel Eliot Morison. This aside, he still praised the movie because it showed "the battle that established beyond doubt the leading role that carriers were to play in the Pacific war."[35] For the viewers of the film, this history lesson not only highlighted the role of aircraft carriers, but also commemorated the Battle of Midway for viewers of all ages.

Paperback Commemoration

An additional form of official commemoration of the entire heritage of the U.S. Navy is seen in paperback books. In the early nineteenth century the expansion of the publishing industry in terms of speed and reduced cost produced an assortment of publications known as the "penny press." This fact altered American history with publishing houses, political parties, and reform movements given the ability to produce informational pamphlets quickly and cheaply. In the next century, paperback books rapidly expanded due to increased overall literacy rates and in part due to needed reading material for American servicemen. After World War II, these cheaply manufactured paperbacks facilitated series of educational books aimed at American youth.

In 1960, the Perennial Library teamed up with *American Heritage* magazine to publish a series of paperback books aimed at a young readership, with topics from American history that included art, maps, and photographs, along with informed scholarship. The editors wrote, "Each book focuses on an outstanding chapter from history—an age made memorable by a great nation, an extraordinary man or woman, a brilliant conquest or discovery."[36] Costing just 75 cents, the series included *Naval Battles and Heroes* and on the front cover a work of art depicts a U.S. Navy man of war under full sail engaged in battle against a flotilla of the British Royal Navy.

The inside cover sets the stage for the interpretative theme of this commemorative paperback. A sketch drawing shows the large aircraft carrier the USS *Yorktown* under fire from Japanese attack. Inset above this scene from World War II are naval heroes Stephen Decatur, George Dewey, and John Paul Jones. Additionally, the work notes that the consultant of the work was a former rear admiral who at the time of publication served as the vice president of the Naval Historical Foundation in Washington, D.C.

In 120 pages the book takes readers from the beginning of nascent U.S. Navy in the American Revolution, to the war with Spain in 1898, and finally the victorious battles against the Axis Powers. Focusing on celebratory aspects of naval heritage, epic battles, and leaders, the work interprets naval history through the lens of bravery and overcoming the odds. More complicated aspects of America's navy heritage, such as the exclusion of Japanese Americans from the service branch during World War II or the segregation of the U.S. military until 1948, are ignored. However, the paperback book not only illustrates an official form of naval commemoration, but also showcases how many young Americans in the postwar period were exposed to the heritage of the U.S. Navy. In short, this salutes the tales of big ships, sailors, and battles, and thus ignores the vast majority of naval history. This is the aim of the work, to boil down the entire experience of the U.S. Navy to just 120 pages for teenage readers.

Iwo Jima

If you drive south on Interstate 10 from Phoenix toward Tucson, you enter a vast expanse of flat desert. Bordered by mountains on the far horizon, it is easy to imagine that most cruise control devices on cars and trucks are engaged as ahead in both directions on the divided highway is straight and appears endless. Most signs on this portion of I-10 are at best glanced at, or more likely ignored, as the one thing that matters for nearly all drivers is the distance to Tucson or Phoenix. One of the first signs leaving Phoenix headed south, however, lists a small community. Exiting at the sign for Sacaton, Arizona, and traveling down Casa Blanca Road, after a few miles you enter the capital of the Gila River Indian Community. A town of just 1,500 people, the civic buildings of Sacaton exhibit handmade artistic recreations of a symbol ubiquitous with American victory in World War II.

This small reservation town in the Sonoran desert bears no connection on the surface with one of the greatest naval operations in history. While it is located on the banks of the Gila River, most days outside of the monsoon season it is bone dry. However, on the library, the local chapter of the American Legion, and in the public park at the only four-way stop in town are artistic reproductions of the famous image taken in February 1945 by Joe Rosenthal of the flag rising on Iwo Jima. The image of five Marines and one U.S. Navy corpsman on top of Mount Suribachi won the Pulitzer Prize for photography. The answer to why this small town holds such a strong connection to the raising of the flag on Mount Suribachi, and by extension the U.S. Marine Corps and the U.S. Navy, is that this was the hometown of one of those Marines in this iconic image. Ira Hayes, a Native American of the Pima tribe, grew up in part on the Gila River reservation.

This small town personifies how a land-based location can serve as a surrogate in naval commemoration. While the island of Iwo Jima certainly is land based, it is a very isolated location in the central Pacific allowing few visitors. In addition, there is no debate that Iwo Jima resides with naval history as every individual Marine, weapon, toothbrush, and meal consumed funneled through the logistical maze of the U.S. Navy. Nearly all these products started in the United States, so while ground fighting was an intricate part of the victory of taking the four-mile wide island, this was a naval operation. In addition, shellfire from surface vessels and ground support from aircraft, all based from warships assigned to the operation, made Marine successes possible.

Sacaton embracing the military heroics of one of its own had impacted the tribal history of the Pima people. This is nothing unique and is seen in nearly all societies. Military service is often shelved with family history. The scholar Joseph Amato addressed this issue in his recent book aimed at rethinking family history. He writes, "Woven of fad and fancy, commerce and technology, war and revolution, freedom and necessity, our individual histories testify to the singular but crooked paths along which we traveled to the present."[37] On this theme, family members of naval veterans can utilize wartime service to connect them to the greater history of the nation. Whether battling the British in the American Revolution or serving on Iwo Jima, families can utilize naval service in connecting to the larger history of the nation-state. More specifically for the amazingly complex Second World War, the personal histories of

Figure 2.3. In Sacaton, Arizona, are many examples, including the local library, of commemorating Ira H. Hayes as one of the individuals raising the flag on Iwo Jima. Photo by Ben Hruska.

Best Practices and Suggestions for Better Interpretation

- Sacaton, Arizona, establishes that commemoration of nationally recognized battles is not dominated by nationally based entities.
- The naming of a library and an American Legion post demonstrate provincial patterns in interpreting naval history.

---

these individual sailors, each just one of millions men and women to serve in the U.S. armed forces during the conflict, connects them to nationally recognized generals, admirals, ships, and battles.

The Election of 1960

The presidential election of 1960, John F. Kennedy verses Richard M. Nixon, pitted two World War II naval veterans against one another. Both were stationed in the South Pacific, both were officers, both witnessed death firsthand, and both used their status as naval veterans in postwar American to enter Congress in 1946. Kennedy, however, possessed one advantage over Nixon in highlighting his service, that of a single vessel's name encapsulating and symbolizing his service. Nixon served on both Green Island and Bougainville, had his tent destroyed in an air raid, and was well liked by the men under his command. He and his men witnessed a wounded B-29 attempting to land and then explode, which he noted in a letter home. Nixon wrote, "I can still see the wedding ring on the charred hand of one of the crewmen when I carried his body from the twisted wreckage."[38] Despite his service, for which he earned two battle stars, Nixon lacked a crystal clear emblem that summed up his service. Kennedy had one with PT 109.

In the inaugural parade for Kennedy, a plywood PT 109 was pulled down Pennsylvania Avenue and naval veterans from the ship waved at their former commanding officer, the newly sworn in president.[39] This combination of two letters and three numbers functioned as a powerful pictogram for his service because it encapsulated the actions of August 2, 1943, when PT 109, with Kennedy at command, was sliced in half by a Japanese destroyer, killing two of the crewmembers. The World War II naval career of JKF shaped the commemoration of the conflict. His rise to the presidency allowed for a reconsideration of the U.S. Navy in World War II as his experience demonstrated that bravery and honor were not limited only to large vessels engaged in massive battles.

In 1961, Robert J. Donovan published *PT 109: John F. Kennedy in World War II*. In early 1963, a film based on the book was released by Warner Brothers, which starred Cliff Robertson as Kennedy.[40] JFK's story commemorated a vessel whose crew consisted of just fifteen men. A reviewer wrote, "In 'PT 109' we see a man assailed by hunger, heat, cold, discouragement and danger rising, without dramatics or pasturing, to greatness."[41] The reviewer believed the story, however, was not limited to JFK. He continued, "The significance is that he was only one of many, only one of a great band of heroes. Our history is bright with those who have risen to the occasion."[42] However, while Kennedy's naval experience helped define his past, and recreational sailing off the coast of New England in a sailboat was his family's love affair, when the U.S. Navy sought a memorial for the fallen president it shunned a small vessel. In April of 1964, Secretary of Defense Robert McNamara ordered the navy to proceed with the plans for CVA 67, which would be named for the murdered president.[43] In memorializing JFK, McNamara sought an aircraft carrier.

The front page of the *New York Times* on May 27, 1967, contained an image of nine-year-old Caroline Kennedy striking a bottle of champagne on the bow of the vessel named for her late father. With her mother and younger brother watching, Caroline declared, "I christen thee John F. Kennedy!"[44] With this centuries-old act, the eighty-eight-thousand-ton monument, in the form of an aircraft carrier for the lost president, rolled back into Chesapeake Bay. President Lyndon Johnson left no doubt about the meaning of this floating memorial in his short dedication. He stated, "Let this ship we christen in his name be a testament that his countrymen have not forgotten."[45] This event on Memorial Day weekend named the vessel, but its formal acceptance into the fleet took place the next year.

Again, on the front page of the *New York Times*, Caroline Kennedy is shown presenting the new captain of the USS *John F. Kennedy*, CVA 67, with a gift of remembrance. She is shown on September 8, 1968, in front of a plaque of a profile of her father.[46] This action demonstrates that the commemoration of Kennedy by the nation was more than simply naming a vessel after a fallen leader. The acceptance and the display of objects onboard related to the thirty-fifth president demonstrates the role vessels played in perpetuating the memory of those for whom they are named. While after World War II the navy outlawed the use of wood on any U.S. Navy vessel in the name of fire suppression, an exception was made for CVA 67. The in-port cabin was designed by Jacqueline Kennedy and used wood paneling, and to honor her husband's love of the sea a framed photograph of Kennedy and his daughter Caroline sailing together was displayed. While Kennedy served during World War II on a vessel whose maximum weight capacity was just over fifty tons, the U.S. Navy remembered him with a large carrier whose complement of sailors numbered in the thousands. In an act of commemoration for a president who was a naval veteran, the dominant force of the fleet was the only adequate memorial.

O'Hare

Other large construction projects in the postwar period came in the form of infrastructure commemorating naval actions in World War II. A chief example of this was the city of Chicago, which in 1949 rechristened not one but two major airports. Both commemorations centered on naval aviation. The first commemorated a naval battle, with the renaming of Chicago's Municipal Airport to that of Midway International Airport.[47] The second honored an individual pilot, Chicago's famed naval aviator Lieutenant Commander Edward H. "Butch" O'Hare.

The latter was originally called Orchard Field and functioned during World War II as a location for aircraft manufacturing. In 1949, the city council of Chicago voted to rename the field in honor of O'Hare.[48] Serving as a naval aviator in early 1942, O'Hare detected a group of Japanese bombers on course to destroy his carrier, the USS *Lexington*, CV 2. O'Hare single-handedly shot down five of these bombers, and in doing so saved his ship and became the first U.S. Navy ace. He was later was awarded the Medal of Honor.[49] While the council's actions in 1949 made the name official, dedication did not take place until 1963. The dedication ceremony included the laying of a wreath in front of a monument to O'Hare by President John F. Kennedy and remarks by the commander in chief, who also served in the navy. Kennedy stated, "His courageous action not only provided a bright spot in the dark days of the Pacific theater, it also helped initiate new techniques of aerial warfare."[50] Noting O'Hare's death later in the war, the president concluded by stating, "but his name lives on in the great international airport we dedicate here today."[51]

British Commemoration: The Battle of Trafalgar

On October 21, 1805, the British Royal Navy defeated Napoleonic France in arguably the greatest sea battle in British history. Of the engagement, the BBC website writes, "the Royal Navy annihilated the greatest threat to British security for 200 years."[52] From the battle a single individual who perished in the fighting rose to near sainthood. Horatio Nelson commanded the entire British force, and while standing on the deck of HMS *Victory* in the heat of battle was struck down by a French bullet. Holding on for a few hours, Nelson kept repeating his motto, "Thank God I have done my duty." The victory destroyed the combined French and Spanish fleet and produced some 1,700 British and 6,000 French and Spanish casualties. Trafalgar after the war set the bar for a nation commemorating a naval battle and a naval commander.

In short, Trafalgar erased the threat of Napoleon invading Britain. While the short dictator from Corsica dominated the continent of Europe, the twenty-two-mile-wide English Channel impeded any plans of crushing the thorn in his side. In 1066, William the Conqueror had led the last successful invasion of the British Isles. After Trafalgar, it was certain that this long span of invasion-free history would continue. Thus, both the commemoration of the battle and the admiral that led it grew exponentially in the decades that followed. In fact, the word *Trafalgar* increased in importance as the true ramifications of the battle played out as the British Empire's power continued to increase. In three commemorative methods, the importance of the legacy of Trafalgar is seen in Nelson's tomb, a public space in London, and the preservation of Nelson's flagship, the HMS *Victory*.

Nelson's Tomb

The location of Nelson's tomb could not be in a more important place in Britain. In the central crypt of St. Paul's Cathedral in the east end of London lies the tomb of Nelson. The most impressive fact of the importance of this exact spot is that it resided vacant for three hundred years waiting for a worthy person, this in an empire with copious amounts of people with amazing military feats and egos to match. Resting atop a gray stone platform, a black sarcophagus holds Viscount Nelson's remains. Situated on top is an amazingly detailed coronet. The site is submerged in naval references. First, the wooden coffin inside the sarcophagus is manufactured from the mainmast of the French vessel *L'Orient*, which was captured at his victory at the Battle of the Nile. The floor around the tomb is covered with depictions of anchors and ropes. On the floor is also the coded message Nelson communicated with signal flags to other vessels of the fleet just before Trafalgar. The brightly colored flags, laid out in a mosaic around the tomb, spells out, "England expects every man will do his duty."[53]

In a sense Nelson became synonymous with Trafalgar itself. In the cathedral that serves as the mother church for the Diocese of London, the seat of the Bishop of London, and on the highest point in the city rests the location for the funerals and burials of the most revered in British society. Funerals that have taken place here have honored Winston Churchill and Margret Thatcher. Also buried in the crypt is the architect of the church, Sir Christopher Wren, and the British hero the Duke of Wellington. In this location, in the place of honor in the crypt directly under the rotunda dome, lays Sir Horatio Nelson.

Trafalgar Square

Walking west out of St. Paul's past the Royal Courts of Justice and into the area known as Covent Garden in a little over a mile and a half is a public space. What Times Square is to New York City Trafalgar Square is to London. From here the National Gallery is a stone's throw away and just down a street to the south are the prime minister's residence, Big Ben, and Parliament. As the largest public square in London, this has been the site since its conception for national celebration and protest. And watching it all from atop a tall column is a statue of Lord Nelson.

Known as Nelson's Column, the 170-foot-tall structure is made of gray stone. At the base is a four-sided pedestal, each with a bronze relief sculptures eighteen feet square in size. All depict naval victories of Nelson's and the symbolism is taken one step further in that all are manufactured from bronze cast from cannons taken from French war vessels. These show artists' renditions of the Battles of Cape St. Vincent, the Nile, and Copenhagen. The fourth panel depicts the death of Nelson at Trafalgar. Nearby water fountains, when running in the warmer months, present an inviting scene for residents and tourists. The square and the battle it commemorates is so central to British identity that Hitler had plans that after the successful invasion and occupation of Britain he would remove Nelson's column and place it in Berlin.[54] This is by far the most visited site commemorating the naval battle of Trafalgar, or any British naval battle for that matter; however, many of those visiting could very well be unaware of the famous engagement. This brings us to the third site marking the battle of the Trafalgar, and certainly represents the most challenging of the three commemorative forms of this section.

HMS *Victory*

Manmade objects and saltwater are engaged in constant conflict, with saltwater winning. The ebb and flow of the tides, storms, and chemical composition of saltwater rapidly deteriorate all stone and metal manipulated by humans in building piers and harbors. For anemic materials like wood, small nails, and tar, such as the hull of the HMS *Victory*, these forces without constant attention will destroy the vessel in a matter of decades. This singular challenge is what faced those preservationists who sought to commemorate Trafalgar with Nelson's flagship. The HMS *Victory* is the location where Nelson was struck down, and when later taken to his cabin, succumbed to his wounds, elevating him to martyr status. This represents a preservationist battle still waged in England to this day, and as long as any piece of Nelson's flagship serves to commemorate the battle, will continue to be fought.

Located at the National Museum of the Royal Navy in Portsmouth, today the HMS *Victory* rests in dry dock. The 104-gun man of war entered service in 1765 and served as a ship of war until 1812, when she then completed a host of auxiliary duties. However, as the decades moved into the nineteenth century, the meaning of her nearly sixty-year career centered solely on October 21, 1805. For Britain, her aging wooden hull functioned as a link to Nelson and the epic battle; however, it remained exposed to the elements and seawater and slowly deteriorated. At the close of World War I, the deterioration had created such as sad state that she was in danger of sinking while tied to the Portsmouth pier. Accordingly, in 1922 she was placed in dry dock.

The official website of the National Museum of the Royal Navy, in utilizing an annotated timeline to outline the history the HMS *Victory* marks her placement in permanent dry dock with "Keeping Up Appearances."[55] By this time her main lower masts made of wood had been replaced with stronger wrought iron masts from a decommissioned vessel from another age. She held just a faction of her originally designed rigging. Her teeth, the cannons that won Trafalgar, were gone, replaced with just a handful of small six-pound guns used in saluting visiting dignitaries or passing vessels. Additionally, the gunports of the hull had been secured with glazed windows, hinting at the hull serving as a ceremonial exhibition piece, not a ship of war. Lastly, other changes, made while she served as a ship and since being housed as a museum piece, had radically changed her appearance. Most notably was a black and white color scheme on the hull added after the War of 1812. Combined, these changes totally transformed what the vessel looked like from the days of Trafalgar. As the museum sites fully notes, "She looks nothing like the ship that Nelson knew at Trafalgar."[56]

Preservationists estimate that today only 20 percent of the wood in the vessel was part of the ship Nelson sailed. Like Lenin's body on display in Red Square, the HMS *Victory* is dead. Both the HMS *Victory* in dry dock and the embalmed body of Vladimir Lenin serve as commemorative symbols for abstract concepts, such as democracy or Christianity that cannot be physically held in your hands. Lenin embodies the founding of a communist socialist republic replacing the Romanov Dynasty and the *Victory* symbolizes a defining naval battle in British history. The sea swallowed all manmade objects and human victims jettisoned overboard during the battle just days after Trafalgar and nothing tangible remained to mark the site. Thus, the *Victory* is the only palpable connection. For British society, she has come to symbolize much more than the worth of wood, rope, and metal of which she is composed.

She is the oldest commissioned warship of any nation. And as a key piece to the legacy of Great Britain's naval heritage, her majesty's government in 2011 devoted $25 million to her restoration. While previous restoration efforts have been piecemeal, this current effort is the single largest attempt at rehabilitation. The scale of the project is massive. Much of the work involves incorporating specialized skills of traditional woodworking with hand tools in carving and shaping wood. Even in the wake of the financial downfall of 2008, in a time of austerity in the United Kingdom, Britain's Ministry of Defense saw her preservation as critical. In terms of British identity, this vessel functions as an indispensable link to the glory of the former empire, and because the empire is no more, her preservation is of critical importance. As John O'Sullivan, project manager of the restoration, said, "If we don't do the work, eventually we'll lose what we've got."[57] The 250-year-old vessel, even with the adaptions made since her commissioning, represents a true window into naval engineering. "It's a work of art,"[58] said O'Sullivan. However, he also notes that this effort of commemorating a battle and national heritage with a ship will be never ending. As he noted, "The first five years will be intense, but it's ongoing forever, it needs constant work."[59]

At the intersection of national identity and myth of war lies the commemoration of the 1805 Battle of Trafalgar. A naval battle was Admiral Nelson's crowning achievement against Napoleonic France. It assured Britain would be free from French invasion and that she would survive a single despot running roughshod on the continent. With the tomb of Nelson under St. Paul's Cathedral, with the public space at Trafalgar Square, and with the HMS *Victory* in dry dock at Portsmouth, a trifecta of naval memorialization is seen and all three demonstrate angles of attack in naval commemoration.

Conclusion

This chapter has considered the depth and breadth of naval commemoration, and even this small sample of examples provides insight into the inventive methodology utilized by public historians. In the commemoration of events occurring on the ever-changing ocean, and the fact that naval vessels rarely survive the peace to be preserved, the human imagination improvised. For example, the nation and the U.S. Navy commemorated two presidents who died while in office, one of natural causes and the other murdered in Dallas, with christening of aircraft carriers with their names. Other forms of official commemoration, such as the naming of an international airport and a USPS stamp, demonstrate the shape commemorative forms can take. We also saw the heritage of the largest battleship transformed not into a marker of valor, but of the larger heritage of science and industry interpreted at Yamato Kure Maritime Museum.

A new method of commemoration has surfaced in the past few years. This form is rather radical and surely would have stunned those original preservationists who sought to save the HMS *Victory* into perpetuity. Differing strikingly from the methodology of taking a weapon of war and metaphorically placing it in a Zip-lock bag for all time, this new approach uses the artifact as canvas. This new technique moves away from seeing an artifact as something to be preserved in a perfect state. For example, rather than considering the correct display of a historic aircraft just one dimensionally with a perfectly restored plane, artists are transforming the airframe of old aircraft into a canvas, and by painting, attempting to convey alternative meanings to the heritage of these aircraft. This type of commemoration 2.0 can be viewed at the Pima Air Museum in Tucson.

Located adjacent the Davis-Monthan Air Force Base, the Pima Air Museum is a mecca for anyone interested in military aviation. Besides over two hundred historic aircraft from a host of nations on display, the museum offers daily tours of the famed "boneyard" on the nearby base. Here, lying in neatly organized rows, are the remains of the Cold War, with retired aircraft waiting to be parted out. On the grounds of the museum itself, aircraft are located in four hangers and an outside twenty-acre site. With so many historic aircraft, they have multiple examples of some of the more resilient aircraft that served for decades. This includes the C-47 and the civilian model equivalent the DC-3. In short, this twin-engine aircraft transformed the movement of people, whether these were paratroopers on D-Day or businessmen commuting between Boston and New York City in the 1950s.

The museum has three such aircraft in rather rough condition. While tires and engines are missing, some of the windows remain; however, for visiting artists, these airframes function as a blank canvas to convey feelings of flight or freedom of movement. On the flat surface on the wings normally designed for engine space, an open-mouthed skull is painted in black and white. Across the body, in hues of gray, blues, and greens, are large feathers. The cockpit of the craft has been transformed into the head of a large bird, with large yellow eyes painted over the pilot and co-pilot's windows. These demonstrate experimentation in commemoration on the part of a well-recognized military aircraft museum. To revive the heritage of an aircraft, not by perfectly restoring it and letting it rest behind velvet ropes, but experimenting in new ways of commemorating.

Figure 2.4. The author standing by new forms of commemoration, airframes of C-47s as canvases at the Pima Air and Space Museum in Tucson, Arizona. Photo by Mitchell Koffman.

Notes

1. "Okie From Muskogee," Classic Country Lyrics, http://www.classic-country-song-lyrics. com/okiefrommuskogeelyricschords.html (accessed January 9, 2016).

2. "Home of the USS Batfish," Muskogee War Memorial Park, http://warmemorialpark.org (accessed November 29, 2015).

3. Mircea Eliade, *Cosmos and History: The Myth of the Eternal Return* (New York: Harper and Row, 1959), 43.

4. Joseph A. Amato, *Guilt and Gratitude: A Study of the Origins of Contemporary Conscience* (London: Greenwood Press, 1982), 8.

5. Ibid.

6. Max Boot, *The Savage Wars of Peace: Small Wars and the Rise of American Power* (New York: Basic Books, 2002), 29.

7. "History & Culture," World War II in the Pacific, National Park Service, http://www.nps. gov/valr/learn/historyculture/index.htm (accessed May 28, 2015).

8. Ibid.

9. Ibid.

10. "Arizona's U.S.S. Arizona Memorial," Historical Marker Database, http://www.hmdb.org/ marker.asp?marker=26425 (accessed May 30, 2015).

11. Quoted from exhibition panel, USS *Arizona* Exhibition, Arizona State Capital Museum, Phoenix, Arizona, visited by author April 3, 2015.

12. "Exhibits," Arizona State Library, Archives and Public Records, http://www.azlibrary.gov/azcm/exhibits (accessed May 30, 2015).

13. "Battleship Yamato," World War II Database, http://ww2db.com/ship_spec.php?ship_id=1 (accessed November 8, 2015).

14. "Yamato," Kure Maritime Museum, http://yamato-museum.com (accessed November 8, 2015).

15. Ibid.

16. Ibid.

17. Ibid.

18. "A Living Naval Museum," Battleship Mikasa, http://aroundtokyo.net/blog/2012/10/28/battleship-mikasa/ (accessed November 9, 2015).

19. "Veterans and the Military on Stamps," United States Postal Service, http://about.usps.com/publications/pub528.pdf (accessed November 14, 2015).

20. Ted W. Lawson, *Thirty Seconds Over Tokyo* (Dulles, VA: Brassey's Inc., 1943).

21. Mervyn LeRoy, *Thirty Seconds Over Tokyo*, DVD, 1944 (Los Angeles, Metro-Goldwyn-Mayer, 1999).

22. "Army & Navy," *Time*, October 29, 1945, 26.

23. "National Affairs," *Time*, November 5, 1945, 19–20.

24. Alexander Feinberg, "Mighty Carrier Roosevelt Commissioned by Truman," *New York Times*, October 28, 1945, 1 and 34.

25. Ibid., 34.

26. Ibid.

27. John Bodnar, *Remaking of America: Public Memory, Commemoration, and Patriotism in the Twentieth Century* (Princeton, NJ: Princeton University Press, 1992), 227.

28. Philip D. Beidler, *The Good War's Greatest Hits: World War II and American Remembering* (Athens: University of Georgia Press, 1998), 3.

29. John Keegan, *The Battle for History: Re-Fighting World War II* (New York: Vintage Books, 1995), 66.

30. Navy memorandum, December 19, 1974; *Lexington* to *Cnaira*, Corpus Christi, Texas, December 26, 1974 (DoD).

31. Lawrence H. Suid, *Sailing the Silver Screen: Hollywood and the U.S. Navy* (Annapolis: Naval Institute Press, 1996), 194.

32. Jack Smight, *Midway*, DVD, 1976 (Los Angeles: Universal, 1996).

33. Suid, *Sailing On the Silver Screen*, 196.

34. Vincent Canby, "On Film, the Battle of 'Midway' is Lost," *New York Times*, June 19, 1976, 11.

35. Ibid.

36. Wilbur Cross, *Naval Battles and Heroes* (New York: Perennial Library, 1960).

37. Joseph A. Amato, *Jacob's Well: A Case for Rethinking Family History* (St. Paul, MN: Minnesota Historical Society Press, 2008), xiii.

38. Lance Marrow, *The Best Year of Their Lives: Kennedy, Johnson, and Nixon in 1948* (New York: Basic Books, 2005), 18.

39. Ibid., 189.

40. Robert J. Donovan, *PT 109: John F. Kennedy in World War II* (Fawcett Publications, 1961).

41. John Toland, "A Profile in Courage, a Background of War," *New York Times*, November 19, 1961, BR3.

42. Ibid.

43. Norman Polmar, *Aircraft Carriers: A Graphic History of Carrier Aviation and Its Influence on World Events* (Garden City, NY: Doubleday, 1969), 665.

44. Max Frankel, "Family of Late President and Johnson at Ceremony," *New York Times*, May 28, 1967, 1.

45. Ibid.

46. B. Drummond Ayres Jr., "Carrier Kennedy Is Handed Over to Navy by Caroline," *New York Times*, September 8, 1968, 1.

47. "Battle of Midway Heroes Honored a Chicago Midway Airport," Chicago Department of Aviation, http://www.ohare.com/About/Midway/BattleOfMidway.aspx (accessed October 14, 2011).

48. "History of O'Hare International Airport," Chicago Department of Aviation, http://www.ohare.com/About/History/Default.aspx (accessed October 14, 2011).

49. John B. Lundstrom, *Fateful Rendezvous: The Life of Butch O'Hare* (Annapolis: Naval Institute Press, 1997), 1–2.

50. "Remarks at O'Hare International Airport Dedication, Chicago, Illinois, 23 March 1963," John F. Kennedy Presidential Library and Museum, http://www.jfklibrary.org/Asset-Viewer/Archives/JFKPOF-043-024.aspx (accessed October 14, 2011).

51. Ibid.

52. "Battle of Trafalgar," BBC History, http://www.bbc.co.uk/history/british/empire_sea-power/trafalgar_01.shtml#six (accessed November 30, 2015).

53. "The Tomb of Lord Nelson (1758–1805)," Explore St. Paul's Cathedral, http://www.explore-stpauls.net/oct03/textMM/NelsonTombN.htm (accessed November 30, 2015).

54. "10 Random Facts and Figures about Trafalgar Square," Londontopia, http://londontopia.net/guides/10-random-facts-and-figures-about-trafalgar-square/ (accessed November 30, 2015).

55. "Restoration," HMS Victory: National Museum of the Royal Navy, http://www.hms-victory.com/restoration (accessed December 1, 2015).

56. Ibid.

57. "HMS Victory: World's Oldest Warship to get $25 Facelift," CNN News, http://www.cnn.com/2011/12/05/world/europe/hms-victory/ (accessed December 3, 2015).

58. Ibid.

59. Ibid.

CHAPTER 3

Objects

THIS POWER OF OBJECTS in a historical context increases exponentially the further the objects recede into the past. As seen with small handheld tools from the Apollo 11 moon landing, items just inches long hold the power to connect visitors to larger historical events. Small objects from naval service can similarly take on a remarkable amount of meaning. As can be witnessed at naval reunions, former sailors display artifacts and photographs of their shared experiences. As most war vessels after service are cut up for scrap, veterans construct and utilize their own visual testaments. All of these objects and images aid in what one naval veteran termed *renewing old stories*.[1] Objects not only serve as a means to mark past experiences, but also as ignition points for conversations with those who did and did not experience the naval events memorialized.

The scholar Kristin Ann Hass argues that veterans utilize objects in rich and diverse ways in remembering trauma and conflict. In her work *Carried to the Wall*, Hass analyzes the placement of objects at the Vietnam Veterans Memorial. She suggests that the Wall on the Mall in Washington, D.C., only represents half the monument. The other half she argues is the objects left by visitors, such as coins, playing cards, a Slim Jim, and cans of beer. She writes, "these intensely individuated public memorials forge a richly textured memory of the war and its legacies."[2] While Hass's work centered on a war that produced deep political and cultural divisions in American society and a national memorial symbolizing an entire war, similar acts of memorialization are seen throughout naval history. Objects can remain displayed in homes, only viewed by family and friends, or brought and shared with veterans and their families at reunions. If a ship was lost as the result of a sinking, acts of self-commemoration give veterans a means to express the loss of ship and shipmates. On a larger scale, citizens can also view singular objects that tether them to long ago battles, important victories and defeats, or martyred sailors.

This chapter looks at the capacity of naval objects. Humans have a long history of assigning meaning to objects in marking sacrifice, mourning, and survival. However, with regard to maritime and naval history, objects retain a special power. While sites of land battles can witness preservation and memorialization with statutes and speeches, ocean environs are ever changing. Sites such as the Battles of Hastings and Gettysburg contract sharply with naval engagements. Permanence is not part of the equation for naval battlefields, as within hours of the completion of the battle any remaining oil, debris, or human victims are erased. Naval objects fill this void of meaning. For the violent and sudden experience of sinkings, sailors, with the use of objects, have invented methods to bridge the gap to mourn, remember, and commemorate.

While the concept of naval experiences is full of romance and adventure, in fact the reality, like the very sea itself, is mostly featureless. Little if any tangible artifacts outside those found within the vessel could serve as a testament to the experience at sea for sailors. If these sailors experience harsh trauma while at sea, this can prove problematic because unlike the battles on land, these sailors are adrift with no place for memorialization. Lacking sacred ground, tangible objects from daily life that marked their time at sea morph into objects for recalling service. Souvenirs acquired while seeing other parts of the world can also transform into windows for recollection. For example, U.S. Navy sailors during World War II who experienced liberty in Casablanca traded with the locals for captured items from the German army such as helmets, pistols, and military medals. Tucking such items in their footlockers, these objects were mailed home once stateside. In a sense, sailors during the war acted as their own archivists. Seeking tangible relics from the war, as they themselves were engaged in naval battles that produced little tangible evidence of war, sailors in ports of call near warzones found markets full of North African merchants selling Axis relics from the land fighting. Decades after the war, such objects served as tangible proof of their wartime experiences.

Bells

In maritime history, the bell of a vessel symbolizes the essence of the ship, as this centuries-old naval tool performs a number of functions including marking time, the changing of the watch, and alerting crewmembers to danger. Ceremonial purposes include signaling the transition of command of the vessel and burials at sea. The importance of each as a symbol is reflected by the U.S. Navy retaining all ships' bells after decommissioning. As the official website for the U.S. Navy states, "The bell remains with the ship while in service and with the Department of the Navy after decommissioning."[3] While bells can be loaned to historic sites, such as a museum, said bells remain in the domain of the Department of the Navy. The purpose of this loaning is "to inspire and to remind our naval forces and personnel of their honor, courage, and commitment to the defense of our nation."[4]

Figure 3.1. Self-commemoration is a central component for many naval veterans remembering their service, as seen exhibiting connecting to a naval vessel on hatware. Photo by Ben Hruska.

Block Island, Rhode Island

The symbolic importance of a bell as an object is seen in a small New England community. The bell from a small escort carrier named the USS *Block Island*, CVE 106, once taken from the decommissioned ship, was stored by the U.S. Navy at the Philadelphia Naval Shipyards. In the early 1970s, the small island community of Block Island, Rhode Island, was interested in acquiring the bell of the scrapped vessel the USS *Block Island*. Local historian and resident Maizie Lewis, with the help of Rhode Island senator Claiborne Pell, brought the bell to Block Island and placed it in front of the local chapter of the American Legion. Housed in a park, this triangular piece of land is adjacent to the island's cemetery. The bell was dedicated on May 31, 1971, in a Memorial Day ceremony.[5] For the residents of this island community, this bell symbolized more than just a piece of the former aircraft carrier; it would function as a memorial for all the Block Island servicemen who served from the Revolutionary War through the Vietnam conflict.

In her dedication of the public memorial, Lewis spoke of this new meaning of the bell. Tolling it three times, she spoke to the gathered crowd: "This bell will be symbolic of more than three centuries of our history . . . it will reverberate across our hills, and its echoes resound across our waters, ever in tribute to those island men who gave their lives for our country."[6] For forty years, this bell has been utilized in memorial services and passing funeral processions. A bell from a scrapped vessel functions as an object used by a small community in honoring national holidays and days of remembrance.

USS *Arizona*, BB 39

The symbolic power of ship's bells transcends all vessel types and geographic locations. For a small island community in New England, the bell from a forgotten aircraft carrier symbolized the service of veterans from all wars. On the other side of the nation, on top of the student union of a major university, is an additional bell from another U.S. Navy vessel. It is an object of remembrance for arguably the most remembered vessel of World War II, the USS *Arizona*, BB 39. Sunk as the result of a horrific explosion on the surprise attack on December 7, 1941, at Pearl Harbor, the vessel is commemorated in various methods in both official forms and by individuals. One of the original bells of BB 39, recovered after the attack, is on the campus of the University of Arizona (U of A) in Tucson. Resting atop the student union, the bell links the vessel and the university christened with the same state. It is important to note that this is an active object, not a relic resting in the climate-controlled conditions of a museum locked away from the public. A rope hangs from it seeking to be used.

At the 2014 USS *Arizona* reunion in Honolulu, with just eleven crewmembers of BB-39 remaining, it was decided to cease holding more reunions. However, in the most recent anniversary event marking December 7 in 2015, a ceremonial event was held in Tucson in which two BB 39 sailors did attend, both well into their late nineties. Held in the student union, those in attendance at the event included the members of the U of A's Navy ROTC, family members of BB 39 sailors, and in the front row, seated in wheelchairs, were the surviving sailors Lauren Bruner and Clare Hetrick. After the speeches on the meaning of the seventy-fourth anniversary, the concluding action in closing the ceremony involved Bruner and Hetrick taking an elevator to the top of the building. At the memorial tower, the bell has rested here since 1951, serving as an object of remembrance. It was saved from being melted down in the salvage yards by a member of the University of Arizona's 1927 class.

Rolled off the elevator in their wheelchairs to a position under the bell, both sailors stood up and grabbed the lowered rope. Pulling down together and tolling it eight times, these sailors marked the deaths of eight BB 39 sailors who were Arizona natives. Then they concluded by tolling it two final times, marking the passing of two of the last survivors of the crew since

---

Best Practices and Suggestions for Better Interpretation

- While most vessels are not preserved after their usefulness as weapons subsides, the bells of these vessels increase in symbolic importance.
- Civic entities, such as small towns and large universities, have successfully harnessed this symbolic power and incorporated such bells into public space.

their 2014 reunion. After ringing the bell, Hetrick was asked of the experience. He said, "It was breathtaking."[7] While the mass of the bell is just a minuscule fraction of the total metal found in what was the battleship USS *Arizona*, BB 39, the symbolic power of this object is colossal.

Swallowed by the Sea

The scholar Dominick LaCapra, in *History and Memory after Auschwitz*, addressed the emotional impact victims undergo from experiencing massive mental trauma. Whereas LaCapra explored this notion while dealing with civilians who experienced the Holocaust, his research is applicable to victims of sinkings. Sailors or civilians undergo a series of mental and physical strains, including the realization that their ship was in danger, followed by attempts to get off the ship, and finally, if successful, finding themselves adrift at sea. About experiences such as these LaCapra wrote, "Especially for victims, trauma brings about a lapse or rupture in memory that breaks continuity with the past, thereby placing identity in question to the point of shattering it."[8] For any individual from any timeframe who survived a sinking on the high seas, massive emotional damage was inflicted and many invented their own forms of coping. Many times the handful of objects that survive, such as items worn by survivors, gain symbolic power and can function as a mooring for meaning of an event consisting of chaotic loss.

Simply put, naval veterans assign a great deal of meaning to small objects. This fact is exemplified at ship's reunions of former sailors and their family members. At such events, mixed among coffee cups and beer cans on tables are objects and photographs that members wish to exhibit. Naval reunions can include small handmade panels highlighting the history of their vessel in the hospitality room of the hosting hotel. Veterans pass around scrapbooks to stimulate conversations about the war and various ports around the world while on liberty. Others bring models constructed of their former ship.[9] All these objects and images assist in what one veteran termed *renewing old stories*. However, objects found at reunions demonstrating the significance of the past are not limited to those decades old.

The reunion group surrounding the USS *Block Island*, CVE 21, from its very beginning sought ways to symbolize itself. In 1983, a patch designed to symbolize the USSBIA, which could be sewn onto a shirt or hat, was for sale.[10] Soon after, hats and shirts also were produced and sold at the reunions. Worn by the veterans, these hats and shirts designated membership in the organization. One veteran recalled a Memorial Day parade the group witnessed in Las Vegas, which included a float commemorating the battleship USS *Nevada*, BB 36. Looking over the crowd, he saw all the members of his organization standing in the mass of people around him and across the street wearing their USSBIA material.[11]

USS *Block Island*, CVE 21

Vessels succumbing to the seas are swallowed. The violence can take nearly all including sailors and the vast majority of objects on board. As a noted naval historian wrote, "When a ship sinks, the battlefield goes away."[12] Thus, objects that survive are critical links to survival.

This phenomenon is seen with the loss of the USS *Block Island*, CVE 21, which in May 1944 was sunk off the coast of Africa after receiving three torpedoes from a cornered German U-Boat.

Sailors who survived the sinking spoke of lost items in oral interviews including photographs, lighters, and poker winnings. Other spoke of items purchased on liberty in Casablanca, such as captured German pistols and North African trinkets. Tucked in their footlockers for the voyage, all were lost with the sinking, thus erasing tangible proof of their wartime experience.

Abandoning ship, all they took with them was what they wore, which for some proved remarkably little as they were in the act of showering. Even those fully clothed found their clothing destroyed as a result of swimming in a mixture of combustible fuels leaking from the wounded carrier. Once rescued, most soiled garments were discarded. However, crewmembers sought to keep tangible pieces of their time in the water to serve as testaments to surviving. As a way to document their loss, some of these men took surviving objects and constructed symbols of their sinking experience. Such artifacts served as more than a way to recall the past. For these functioned as a memorial to a lost ship and shipmates.

Hector Vernetti retained two items after abandoning ship: his belt and shoes. After the war, Vernetti heard of a U.S. Army veteran bronzing the boots he wore walking across Europe. Vernetti attempted a similar method with his shoes. Placing plaster of Paris inside his navy-issued shoes, he applied gold paint. Vernetti, like all World War II veterans, was a kid of the worldwide Depression where families survived by wasting nothing. Everything needed a purpose, including handmade memorials. Thus, Vernetti's monument to the sinking also served the useful purpose of doorstops in his home in Scottsdale.[13]

Hector Vernetti served as a parachute rigger on board CVE 21. His position included the packing and repairing of parachutes and working with cloth, silk, thread, and sewing equipment. While at work one day, someone showed up with orders from the commanding officer of the ship to gather supplies—colored pencils, cloth, and needle and thread—to be given to German POWs held on board. With spare time on their hands, these German prisoners made memorials to their lost comrades and U-Boat and a handful were given to the crewmembers of CVE 21. Vernetti received one of these hats as a gift for providing the supplies. This memento of the war produced by the Germans was in Vernetti's footlocker, waiting to be mailed home once stateside, at the time of the sinking. In recalling the loss of his vessel, Vernetti first spoke of this hat locked in this footlocker for safekeeping that sank beneath the waves.[14]

Investigating the history of the USS *Block Island*, CVE 21, demonstrates other objects that over time were donated to a small museum on Block Island, Rhode Island. While formed in 1942 and devoted to preserving the rural farming and fishing history of this island community, the museum cultivated a permanent USS *Block Island* collection over time. One of the more unique objects donated was a German hat manufactured by a crewmember of a lost U-Boat. A German survivor who was held prisoner on the USS *Block Island* made the hat of white cloth in the fashion of what is termed an "overseas hat." On one side in black ink is a surfaced U-Boat, above which is a swastika. The opposite side has a date, March 17, 1944, noting the loss of his particular U-Boat, U 801. Situated near the date are the names Schulz, Toller, Helbig, and Neubauer, all lost comrades that perished with the destruction of the vessel.[15]

Figure 3.2. Hector Vernetti shows this homemade memorial to surviving the sinking of his vessel, which he constructed from the shoes worn abandoning ship. Photo by Ben Hruska.

CVE 21 on missions seeking to find and destroy German U-Boats in the Atlantic served as the head of a task force that was composed of smaller vessels. In the course of destroying U-Boats, German survivors at times would be recovered, and with operations lasting upward of a month, surviving U-Boat crews were transferred to the larger USS *Block Island*. This allowed for the intelligence officer on board to interview these crewmembers for any valuable information on their particular U-Boat or the nature of the Atlantic war in general. Until the task force resupplied, in either Casablanca or Norfolk, these Germans POWS resided on the ship.[16]

The make-up of the crews sheds light onto the nature of the conflict. In January 1944, CVE 21 received prisoners from U 231. The Germans brought on board were segregated into officers, noncommissioned officers, and enlisted men to prevent communication between these groups in the hopes of improving the information gathered from interrogations. Most of the officers could speak English at an intermediate, and some at a higher, level. One of first requests of the commanding officer of U 231, Captain Wenzel, was to remember his lost crew. During interrogation he asked in English, "I wonder if it would be possible for us to have a memorial service for our departed comrades."[17]

The USS *Block Island* chaplain, Lieutenant Gordon A. MacInnes, held three separate services, each for the three segregated units. The services included "a short opening prayer,

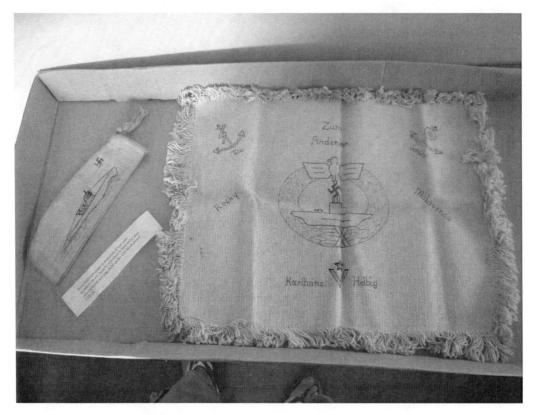

Figure 3.3. German veterans from U-Boats constructed memorials to their lost ship and ship-mates after capture, which they traded with American sailors for cigarettes. Photo by Ben Hruska.

a portion of the usual verses from the Bible, which are read at funerals, and longer, final prayer."[18] MacInnes spoke in English and a junior grade officer translated the statements into German. With no bodies of their former comrades to mourn over, this was the nearest form of closure for the Germans to say goodbye to their dead shipmates.

The loss of a ship, and the death of crewmates, produced strong feelings that many of the victims found difficult to express verbally. The anthropologist Fabio Gygi explores the experiences of World War I veterans seeking closure with the use of war objects. According to Gygi, "We give meaning to our experiences not only through language but also by putting them into some order, whose origin is a spatially constructed model of reality."[19] Vernetti or the Germans who lost their U-Boat, in recalling losing their vessel on the high seas, discussed objects lost and not individual feelings. They spoke of a wallet with money left on a table, images with buddies while in port, and letters from home. Such objects take on a symbolic power and decades after the war provide clarity. One of the greatest challenging concepts for survivors maybe the emotions around understanding the randomness of their survival, and perhaps knowing that the object, like themselves for whatever reason, also survived, offers victims of sinkings some peace of mind in the irregularity of war.

The previously mentioned German hat that was donated to the Block Island Museum lacked the original accession information, which would note the giver, date of the donation, and the contact information of the giver. Despite lacking this critical information, the object still represents a duel act of remembering. First, the object demonstrates the construction of a memorial by a German POW struggling to deal with the loss of his U-Boat and crewmembers. Second, the donation shows the act of preservation for this piece of USS *Block Island* history. Whether the donation was from a veteran or a family member of a veteran, this action of seeking a home for the object in perpetuity highlights the giver's need of placing this artifact from CVE 21 into the larger understanding of the war. This action shifted the object from the domain of the individual to that of a museum.

Donations to a small local museum anchored these veterans' artifacts to a specific place. They adopted a local museum, rather than a large national or regional institution, to serve as a safe harbor for their memories and objects. Joseph Amato theorizes on the meaning of local history to a community, and in this case a community of veterans scattered across a country. He writes, "Local history satisfies an innate human need to be connected to a place. It feeds our hunger to experience life directly and on intimate terms."[20] For an expanded community of naval veterans lacking a specific land-based location, the avenue of local history for their ship's namesake was selected for the preservation of not only their memories, but also their material culture.

Booi's Skivvies

Joe Booi kept his skivvies (navy slang for underwear) after the sinking of CVE 21 and brought these to reunions to show his fellow shipmates and others. Booi's last name and first initial are on the top of the garment. Even after seventy years, when one touches Booi's skivvies, oil and fuel comes off onto the holder's hands. Besides serving as a visual testament to the ordeal, the object also affects the sense of smell. Abandoning ship, the sailors were engulfed in combustible fuels leaking from their wounded vessel; this object hints as to the conditions of the seas for the survivors.[21] Booi first sought to keep his skivvies as proof of his ordeal, then later he brought these to reunions for others to see. Finally, nearing the end of his life and battling cancer, Booi donated the skivvies to the USS *Block Island* collection.

The construction of works of art also functioned as a visual marker to the demise of CVE 21.[22] Sailor Rudy Bowling's sketch depicting the sinking shows the bow of the USS *Block Island* unnaturally high in the air, revealing a massive hole from a torpedo strike. Attached to the mast of the fast sinking ship is a U.S. flag fully extended by the wind, soon to be swallowed by the Atlantic. In the sea around the vessel, tiny figures swim away from the fate of the vessel. On the horizon, friendly U.S. Navy vessels are en route to rescue swimming sailors. Lastly, in the sky above, blended with the clouds, is a roped Jesus Christ with a bowed head as he watches over those in danger in the water. Bowling considered his work a communal experience as he shared it with others who also experienced the event at USS *Block Island* reunions.[23] His illustration uses art to attempt to understand this remarkable event from a communal past. A copy of Bowling's work ended up being donated to the greater USS *Block Island* collection.

Figure 3.4. Sailor Joe Booi donated his skivvies saturated in fuel oil after the sinking of the USS *Block Island*, CVE 21, to a larger museum collection of objects related to his ship. Photo by Ben Hruska.

In gathering artifacts, public historians can look beyond just individual veterans and their organizations. Family members of veterans also represent a huge potential for acquiring objects for short-term loans or outright donation. Ken Vachon donated his deceased father's U.S. Navy dress blues, which were issued to his dad when he joined the navy, for an exhibition on the USS *Block Island*. This uniform retains a link to his father's service in a number of ways, including showcasing his rank on the sleeve. The slenderness of the uniform demonstrates that the original wearer of the piece was a young man, not fully grown into adulthood, and also hints at the age of some sailors as young as fifteen.[24]

Vachon decided to donate his father's uniform after hearing the news of an upcoming exhibit on his father's ship. In the accession records, Vachon noted the trimness of the uniform issued to his seventeen-year-old father.[25] His family thus entrusted his deceased father's tangible connection to his military service to a larger collection of material related to the story of his father's ship. As Vachon wrote, "Our family would be pleased and honored to donate them, in his memory to the Block Island Museum."[26] Displayed in an exhibition, this uniform connected one more family to the museum in the short term with an exhibition, but also in the long term with the permanent USS *Block Island* collection.

The donation highlights opportunities for public historians in gaining the trust of individuals, civic organizations, and local leaders. Historic organizations of all kinds can look to increase public awareness in harnessing trust from those seeking an organization to house their own personal history. This potential is seen in veterans and family members donating tangible connections to naval service to a local museum on Block Island. Family history and the benefits of museums engaging in it are not just limited to small local historical societies. While normally in the realm of local history, this is a neglected aspect for many medium and large institutions and holds a huge potential for public historians with all topics, not just naval related.

The author Joseph Amato argues that these personnel items, such as a service uniform, are better suited for local history as opposed to those telling a national story. He writes, "Only local and regional history satisfies the need to remember the most intimate matters, the things of childhood."[27] Amato's theme is clearly seen with items related to a sinking as the range of objects including uniforms, skivvies, and German-made memorial caps. Thus, the adoption of the local history provided those donating a platform for remembering. However, historians of naval topics can locate connections on numerous levels including the individual, state, and regional. We can challenge the notion that local history only resides in the small town historical society. All locations, no matter how dense in population or how cosmopolitan, possess connections to the local. Objects allow us to latch onto that powerful force of local history.

Best Practices and Suggestions for Better Interpretation

- In naval interpretation, naval veterans and their families assign a massive amount of meaning to objects.
- With interpretation of any objects, it is hard to overstate the importance of the province of the artifacts. This should encourage curators accepting objects to acquire all possible information in the accession process.
- In the commemoration of their wartime experiences, veterans reserve the right to transform original objects to create and assign meaning.

Vessel as Object

While individuals seek out objects for meaning, the same is true with the navies of the world. One of the oldest forms of commemorating the heritage of a ship was not the actual preservation of wood, iron, or steel, but the rechristening of an additional vessel, or transferring the fighting heritage of a vessel and sailors onto another vessel. An ancient practice, the U.S. Navy adopted this technique from its founding in 1775. For example, the World War II–era fast fleet carriers, such as the USS *Hornet*, CV 8, and the USS *Wasp*, CV 7, represent a link in the chain of U.S. Navy heritage of nomenclature from the eighteenth century. Both were lost in

1942 and new carriers were rechristened the next year with the USS *Hornet*, CV 12, and the USS *Wasp*, CV 8.[28] While this transference of legacy from ship to ship bodes well for naval heritage, it takes its toll on the physical vessels as these become expendable. It is so easy to remove the historical value of a vessel because little stands in the way of recycling a rusting decommissioned hull. Similar to a merry-go-round, the newly commissioned vessels that earn a legacy-rich title such as *Wasp* decades later are easily stripped of this heritage.

The first USS *Wasp*, purchased as a merchant schooner, entered service in 1776 and joined the war for American independence against the British Navy. Subsequent U.S. Navy vessels retained the heritage of the first *Wasp*.[29] In World War II, with the loss of the USS *Wasp*, CV 7, the navy immediately made plans for an additional aircraft carrier to continue this proud name. Fletcher Pratt, a naval commentator, wrote of this transfer of legacy while the war still waged. He wrote, "So the *Wasp* is gone, and now there is a new *Wasp* under construction."[30] He stressed the transferability of heritage from the old *Wasp* to the new aircraft carrier with "she will be a dangerous ship, but more dangerous to the enemy than to those aboard, and those who served on the old *Wasp* are eager to be on the new."[31] While the navy can officially mark the loss of a vessel with a replacement, for the men who experienced the violence first-hand, dealing with the loss is much more personal and thus problematic. While the navy lost a vessel, they lost fellow crewmembers.

USS *Franklin*, CV 13

Citizens of New York City toward the end of World War II witnessed a massive blackened and burned object docked on the waterfront that showcased the naval war in a unique role. The heavily damaged vessel, the USS *Franklin*, CV 13, was within fifty miles of mainland Japan when an undetected enemy fighter dropped two bombs on the vessel. The explosions and later fires and other interior explosions killed 724 crewmembers. While the damage threatened the existence of the vessel, her crew saved her and later towed her to Pearl Harbor for basic structural repairs. Once completed, the charred carrier returned to the mainland United States under her own power for planned restoration.[32] However, the navy had another role for her before complete restoration took place.

Named by the crew as "The Ship That Wouldn't Die," the USS *Franklin* served as a singular object on the Pacific war for the American public.[33] The scholar Alison Landsberg wrote of the power of museums, which includes the use of objects, to affect the perspective of those who had no firsthand knowledge of a particular experience. She wrote, "The museum, like the comic book, raises questions about what it means to own or inhabit a memory of an event through which one did not live."[34] The American public had followed the Pacific war through newspapers, radio reports, and staccato newsreel film clips shown before feature films. Such reports included the costs of war, men who did not return home alive, ships lost, and planes shot down. However, seeing the costs of war, such as a violently damaged ship, was limited, for the most part, to black-and-white images and movie clips. Seeing the actual damage inflicted on the USS *Franklin*, which floated in the harbor of New York, brought the war home in a visual way in a completely new form.

Arriving in New York on April 28, 1945, she docked in Brooklyn and her heavily damaged condition brought the war home. As a report described the USS *Franklin*, "her main mast lean[ed] at a sharp angle, her foremast a jagged stump, her steel plates buckled and torn and her flight deck completely destroyed."[35] She was opened to the public for inspection and crowds walked on her flight deck in awed fascinated on both the Navy Day celebrations of 1945 and 1946.[36]

The damage witnessed by these noncrewmembers, her charred hull and heavily damaged flight deck, symbolized more than just twisted metal; it also brought to mind the 724 sailors who perished onboard. However, the damage inflicted on this object also showed the resilience of the U.S. Navy, as an issue of *All Hands* noted for its armed service readers. It stated that the ship offered "a tribute to the spirit of the officers and bluejackets who man the Navy's fighting ships, this 'Fighting Lady' stayed afloat as others have similarly survived through the heroism of those who manned them."[37] She served as an early object granting insight into the U.S. Navy's war in the Pacific. This twisted vessel nullified distance in terms of both geography and experience. For American civilians, walking on this object transformed newspaper headlines into a personal connection.

Ancient History

In 1954, the Egyptian archeologist Kamal el Mallakh led a dig near the south side of the Great Pyramid at Giza. After removing topsoil, the team found a layer of charcoal, woodchips, and powdered limestone, and below this forty perfectly carved limestone blocks laid in a rectangle. Placing an exploratory hole, an open chamber was discovered and el Mallakh peered inside. What he smelled first, and not saw, is what grabbed his immediate attention because the aroma of the chamber was cedar, which does not grow in Egypt. Flashlights beaming light inside revealed a wooden vessel and oars. From the very beginning it was clear that this discovery would cause a reevaluation of the early timeline of Egyptian history. In fact, it produced a debate that still goes on today on the purpose of this vessel.

Today at the foot of the Great Pyramid stands a rectangular building. The purpose is to protect and display the forty-six-centuries-old vessel found entombed below this location to honor Khufu, the pharaoh responsible for constructing the Great Pyramid. The 144-foot-long vessel is called today the "solar boat." Removing the vessel from the burial chamber was a herculean effort and after twenty months the vessel was deassembled into 1,200 pieces and successfully reassembled at the current site. The pharaoh's craftsmen, utilizing cedar most likely brought in from present-day Lebanon, produced a craft resembling a puzzle with the main hull consisting of thirty planks, some of which are over seventy-five feet long. Additionally, all twelve oars are carved from a single piece of wood. Using only copper and flint tools, workmen over four thousand years ago constructed a vessel that in terms of craftsmanship rivals any boat manufactured today. However, the vessel raises the question of the intended purpose.

This vessel serves as an object challenging the established timeline of ancient Egyptian history. While it brought context to the Great Pyramid at Gaza, it simultaneously produced bigger questions. Fifty years after the discovery, debate among experts on the purpose of the craft range from it being a funerary craft used in transporting Khufu's body to be entombed to it being simply a symbolic craft to be used in voyages across the skies for the deceased. On a Public Broadcasting Service (PBS) show, Nova states, "Over a half a century after the boat's discovery . . . its function remains an enigma."[38] For those interpreting naval history, it demonstrates the use of a vessel as an object to challenge preconceived notions of the past stretching back four thousand years. As a single object, this Egyptian example starts this section on analysis of the multiple symbolic forms stationary vessels at rest can take on.

Aurora

Commissioned in 1900, this cruiser was constructed by the Russian Empire and named by Czar Nicholas II after the Roman goddess of Dawn. She first saw action in the Russo-Japanese War of 1904–1905. Sailing at a top speed of nineteen knots, she cruised to battle in the Pacific by heading west away from St. Petersburg and out into the Baltic Sea, south around the Horn of Africa, and then traversed the Indian Ocean. Assembling with the Russian armada, the Japanese Navy destroyed the Russian fleet in a matter of minutes. The *Aurora* was one of only four Russian ships to survive. However, the true fame around the *Aurora*, in which she would be transformed into a symbol of revolution, and the sole reason she exists today, came in the next decade.

For the Russian Empire, the year 1917, with the costly three-year involvement in World War I, was a year of chaos. The Romanov dynasty that ruled for centuries was removed and two vying forces sought control. The "White" Provisional Government sought a democratic government based on Western European models for the future Russia, while the "Red" Bolsheviks wanted a Communist state. In October 1917, the White forces appeared to have the upper hand with control of the symbol of Romanov power, the Winter Palace in St. Petersburg. However, the Reds led a successful storming of the palace, and mythology after the event chronicled that the sailors of the *Aurora* fired a blank charge from her large guns as a signal to commence the attack. While historians today still debate the link between the discharge of the *Aurora*'s guns and the attack on the Winter Palace, in terms of Soviet mythology after successfully establishing the Union of Soviet Socialist Republics, the *Aurora* embodied the October Revolution.

The single largest step in the Bolsheviks elevating the cruiser to a mythical level took place in the filming of the movie *October* in 1927. Filming both on board the *Aurora* and on location on the River Neva where she fired the blank charge provided a manufactured visual testament of the start the October Revolution. This visual testament of the *Aurora* reenacting the act, and shown in cinemas across the USSR, solidified her position as an icon of Bolshevism. The Soviets, in a brilliant production of national identity, crafted a unique visual testimony in myth making, a true instance of a nation-state making a legend out of a vessel a decade after the event. With the use of total state control and movie-making technology, the USSR "recreated" a myth of their own making with the use of a vessel as central actor and subject.

In World War II, the *Aurora* would assist in victory by symbolic means rather than military successes battling the Nazis. In the nine-hundred-day siege of Leningrad, her guns were removed and used to shell the German enemy that surrounded the city as she lay docked. However, even without a crew and means to fight, her mast never took down the Soviet flag. Again, as an icon she boosted morale for a population undergoing the worst siege in history in which a million residents died of hunger and cold.

In the decades after World War II, she remained docked in Leningrad and served as a training ship and dormitory for the Nakhimov Naval School. When the school expanded to house all its cadets, the *Aurora* morphed into a museum to herself and the revolution she spawned according to Soviet doctrine. Even after the collapse of the USSR, and the influences of the West poured in, including Western tourists, the mystique of the cruiser remained. As a Russian reporter wrote, "A visit to the legend of the Russian fleet was an important part of any tourist itinerary, and during the Soviet period the ship held an almost religious standing as the most important symbol of the Bolshevik Revolution."[39] At the time of this writing, full restoration of the *Aurora* has just taken place for the one-hundredth anniversary of the October Revolution. Of this rebooting of an object, the same Russian reporter noted, "Museum employees say that it will now be dedicated to the evolution of shipbuilding and the Russian fleet, rather than the revolutionary events of 1917."[40] The *Aurora* demonstrates the theme of adaptability seen in naval warfare and commemoration. Built by a feudal empire, she gained fame later under a state based on Marxist theories. Participating in a revolution, and the young nation-state knowing the importance of a population needing heroes to embody national ideals, the *Aurora* transformed from a platform of war into a platform of memory.

Hangor

From the German use of U-Boats in the Battle of the Atlantic to the American use of subs in breaking the back of the Japanese Empire's maritime shipping, the submarine played a critical role in World War II. While the concept was old, technology had finally caught up with naval imagination in the early twentieth century. Proportionally, these relatively small craft decimated surface ships, as attested to by a single submarine being able to sink tens of thousands of tons of enemy vessels. With thousands of skeletons of vessels rusting on the bottom of the world's oceans attesting to the lethal nature of submarine warfare, it is a bit surprising that after the Second World War it would be twenty-five years before another submarine scored a kill. Another surprise is the context around this action. The two participating nation-states, both victor and vanquished, did not legally exist the last time a submarine sank a vessel. The Indian-Pakistan War of 1971 stemmed from Great Britain giving up control of British India in 1947, and the division of religion fractured the colonial holding into India, Pakistan, and Bangladesh. Tensions ebbed and flowed between India and Pakistan and in 1971 turned into a shooting war. The regional tension followed predictable Cold War lines, with the United States and the Soviet Union backing rival factions and the conflict lasting less than a month. While India won, Pakistan achieved one victory at sea over a much larger and formidable Indian Navy (INS) to rally around and celebrated after the brief war.

Hangor translates into "shark," and the Pakistani Navy purchased the newly manufactured submarine from France. At the start of the conflict, it was just under a year old and the diesel-powered submarine went out to confront a superior Indian Navy. With India control-ling of the skies with aircraft, the *Hangor* could only remain submerged in the daylight hours and seek to achieve a favorable attacking position. After a thirty-hour approach, the *Hangor* fired a torpedo at the anti-submarine frigate the INS *Khukri*, and the explosion broke the vessel nearly in two. It sank in two minutes, killing all hands. But the ordeal of the "Shark" was just beginning, as other Indian vessels joined a massive hunt seeking to destroy her, during which the INS reported the *Hangor*'s destruction more than once. Surviving hours of evading detection and over one hundred depth charges dropped on the lone Pakistani submarine, the *Hangor* pulled back into Karachi as a victor. The fact that the nation lost the war made the success of the *Hangor* all the more important.[41] A smaller, less powerful nation took on a stronger and larger enemy and survived. And when her service life ended in 2006, she would metamorphose into an object of nation triumph.

The symbolic importance of this object to the nation-state of Pakistan is seen at its ded-ication, with the main speech conducted by Chief of the Naval Staff Admiral Mohammad Afzal Tahir. The theme of his speech centered on the four-decade-long transformation of the Pakistani Navy from a nascent collection of small ships manned by brave sailors into the strong force it is today. As he stated, "Today's occasion also reminds us of the responsibilities and the trust reposed by our nation for the maritime defense of the country in us."[42] Standing adjacent to the *Hangor*, the naval chief paid tribute to her 1971 crew in attendance. After the events of December 9, 1971, the submarine became synonymous with victory over India. While her hull and technology are dated and unfit for warfare in the twenty-first century, her mission is far from over. On display at the Pakistan Maritime Museum, visitors walk inside her, see the periscope that spotted the Indian enemy, and see the tubes that launched the torpedoes. Of the *Hangor*, the naval chief said, "It will act as an aesthetic interface between the Navy and the public and will certainly inspire and education the younger generation."[43]

While the Indian-Pakistan War of 1971 was a strategic loss for Pakistan, the *Hangor* overcoming the odds and sinking an anti-submarine frigate of the Indian Navy fit well into the classic narrative of David and Goliath. While a stronger and better organized India won the month-long war, Pakistan survived, and the single greatest event to demonstrate this resil-ience is that Pakistan scored the first successful submarine kill of any nation in twenty-five years. Thus, while the Pakistani Navy retired the *Hangor* from active duty in the Indian Ocean, she still cruises on in a new stationary mission in Karachi in representing victory over India.

USS *Pueblo*

On January 23, 1968, an incident occurred off the coast of North Korea that for a brief period brought worldwide fear of the Cold War heating up exponentially. North Korean sea and air forces surrounded and boarded a vessel of the U.S. Navy. For the first time in over a century and a half, a foreign power successfully captured a U.S. Navy ship. At the time, the USS *Pueblo*, AGER 2, was gathering intelligence in international waters; however, North Korea disputed the location of the incident. Once taken into custody, the USS *Pueblo* and the eighty-two surviving crewmembers were transported to North Korea. With the United States already bogged down in one land war in Asia and remembering the costly war on the Korean peninsula in the early 1950s, diplomacy prevailed rather than the use of military might. While the crew suffered harsh conditions and beatings, after 355 days they were released two days before Christmas. The prize of the USS *Pueblo* remained, however, and to this day is the only commissioned U.S. Navy ship in the possession of another nation.[44]

In 2013, the USS *Pueblo* served as a centerpiece in North Korea celebrating the sixtieth anniversary of what it termed "Victory Day," which marks the conclusion of the Korean War. Sporting a coat of freshly applied gray paint and docked in the Pothong River, the USS *Pueblo* served as the physical embodiment of the nascent Communist state taking on the United States. As the *Guardian* reported in 2013, "The ship is North Korea's greatest cold war prize, a potent symbol of how the country has stood up to the great power of the United States, once in an all-out ground war and now with its push to develop nuclear weapons and sophisticated missiles."[45] After the Victory Day event, it remained on public display at the Fatherland War of Liberation Museum. Images found online show North Korean troops reviewing the vessel and the North Korean leader Kim Jong Un receiving a personal tour. Photos from the side facing the museum show a pristinely painted USS *Pueblo*; however, views from the river of the starboard side are quite different and not shown on North Korean–run state media outlets because it shows the rust and deterioration accumulating from neglect, hinting at the dubious aspects of a closed society where any form of questioning of the Supreme Leader, who is the state, is an act of dissent. Once again, this example from North Korea exemplifies an additional form a retired vessel can take. As a Cold War prize, the USS *Pueblo* exhibits surviving the joint attacks by the United States and the United Nations during the Korean War for the state of North Korea, and also later taking on the U.S. Navy gathering intelligence off her shores.

"Quite Independent of Place"

The historian Stephen Pyne, in writing of the nature of ships, wrote a short passage that sums up the fundamental difficulty of understanding the history of any particular vessel. He writes that ships are "quite independent of place."[46] This short sentence underlines the challenge in understanding a large manmade object that in its very nature is kinetic, never stationary, besides periodic stops in faraway ports. Whether the wooden inventions crafted by Vikings from Baltic forests powered by oars and sail or modern vessels that measure in the hundreds of feet long and as large of any stadiums of the ancient world, these are designed around action and movement. In rare instances, retired vessels earn a second life as a cultural destination, for the first time inheriting a particular place.

For a handful of vessels that survived the wars, bold captains, and typhoons, a variety of entities reformulated a mobile warrior into a stationary ambassador. For these rare vessels, if successfully framed as a symbolic object larger than the wood or metal composing the ship, only then do these take on another cultural mission. As seen in diverse locations such as ancient Egypt, Pakistan, Bolshevik Russia, and North Korea, ships as symbolic objects can convey a range of state-sponsored meaning. Understanding this metamorphosis that occurs

- These examples demonstrate the range of meaning that can be assigned to former ships of war including naval victory, national origin, and chronicling a triumph of a nation-state.
- That in completing such interpretation, much latitude is granted to those in charge of the interpretation.
- That interpretation is subject to change. As Bolshevik Russia evaporated, the importance of the *Aurora* did not dissipate. The replacement nation-state reinvented a new meaning for its citizens for the floating ambassador to the past.

from an aging ship deviating into symbolic artifact will give those interpreting naval topics a window in grasping these examples of mooring of memory. These ships serve as a stationary metaphor and not a mobile wayfarer.

Philippine Pilgrimage

While nations can rechristen a carrier, battleship, or cruiser to remember a vessel lost in naval combat, individual family members and surviving crewmembers feel a need to developed more intimate methods of remembrance. While a replacement vessel completes commemoration for the nation-state, steel forming a new vessel does little to help heal the scars of individual sailors. Additionally, families of the lost are at a disadvantage in means to construct a large-scale memorial such as an additional war vessel. A quick sinking takes away the ship and victims as the ocean swallows all. However, one particular group of survivors deserves the attention of public historians in that they invented an object to bridge the gap created with the loss of their World War II vessel.

Survivors utilize objects in obtaining closure. One cohort of World War II sailors manufactured a symbolic object, and combined with years of long-term planning, were able to host a unique ceremony on the very site of their sinking off the coast of the Philippines. Hosting a ceremony remembering tragedy on the open ocean is saturated with obstacles. However, crewmembers of the carrier the USS *Gambier Bay*, CVE 73, did accomplish this feat. For those involved in naval history, their pilgrimage overcoming decades of time and the logistics of visiting the site in the Philippine Sea grants a window into the inventive nature of the use of objects in naval remembrance.

A task force of the U.S. Navy named Taffy 3, composed of six escort carriers and other smaller vessels, on October 25, 1944, was taken by surprise by a massive Japanese fleet that included four battleships, six heavy cruisers, and eleven destroyers. The lightly armored escort carriers faced an incredible amount of firepower from the Japanese fleet's heavy guns, and they bravely fought a retreating battle. Planes from the small carriers attacked the enemy while the escort carriers attempted to stay out of range of the massive Japanese guns. The sailors of Taffy 3 showed stunning courage, which was chronicled by the historian Samuel Eliot

Morison. He wrote, "In no engagement of its entire history has the United States Navy shown more gallantry, guts and gumption that in those two morning hours between 0730 and 930 off Samar."[47] This battle came with major costs, including the loss of two CVEs. The USS *St. Lo*, CVE 63, sunk as a result of a single kamikaze hit, while the USS *Gambier Bay*, CVE 73, earned a unique footnote in naval history. With her comparatively paper-thin hull, the massive Japanese shells tore the vessel apart, and she became the only carrier in history lost to naval gunfire.

While the majority of the crew of the *Gambier Bay* abandoned ship and survived, as they floated for two days in shark-infested waters, the loss of their ship and crewmembers created a massive emotional shock. One veteran recalled making a pledge to himself while in the water watching his stricken vessel. He wrote, "While swimming away from my sinking ship, I made a vow to some day return to the site where the USS Gambier Bay lies at the bottom of the Philippine Trench. This trip would be to honor our Killed in Action with a religious and military memorial service."[48] Where the circumstances of the battle did not permit a funeral for those deceased crewmembers, in the decades after the war the men of the USS *Gambier Bay* returned to the site and held a fitting ceremony. Taking over thirty years to come to fruition, returning to the site of the sinking included the dropping of a specially constructed object to descend on their wrecked carrier seven miles below the surface.

In St. Louis, the first official USS *Gambier Bay* reunion took place in 1969 with a core goal of completing the pilgrimage. As one organizer wrote, "The pledge was to return to bury the dead with prayers to God and their souls and to afford a military burial with full honors."[49] Over the course of reunions, the plan evolved for the visitation to the location to coincide with the anniversary of the loss.

In October 1977, the return trip to the Philippines took place. While their trip included two weeks of events and visits to sites of American and Filipino military importance, they came to honor lost shipmates thirty-three years after their deaths. The logistics of the trip required a driven personality, the president of the Philippines Ferdinand Marcos, who aided with the loaning of his personal yacht to visit the exact coordinates of the sinking, allowing the one hundred people in attendance to be on a single vessel for the service. On October 25, 1977, the ship, loaded with veterans, family members, and a Filipino honor guard, came to rest on the sinking site. Silence enveloped the congregation as the engines quieted and the ocean's large swells rocked the yacht. A former crewmember broke the silence by speaking aloud, "They're telling us that they know we're here and they appreciate that we have come to keep our vow. Now they can rest in peace. They're kicking up the sea from below."[50]

The former chaplain of the USS *Gambier Bay* led the service, which included reciting the Lord's Prayer and singing religious hymns. After the name of a sailor who died was read aloud, a red carnation was placed in the water and a member of the Filipino honor guard fired his rifle. These actions mirrored traditional military funerals that transpire on land, whether the family members have the deceased body or not. However, an additional component of the memorial service was the placement of an object to sink and come to rest below them in the Philippine trench.

Before the service, a round capsule, with "USS *Gambier Bay*" on the side, was filled with offerings. Items to be transported down by the capsule included personal objects from shipmates and family members, including American flags donated by veterans' organizations. Also, in a symbol of the alliance between the United States and Filipinos during the war, an American and a Filipino flag were folded together and sealed into the capsule with the other objects before slowly descending through the blackness and miles of saltwater onto the site of whatever remained of the USS *Gambier Bay*.

Before concluding, the service allowed for individual veterans to speak. One veteran stood up and noted that thirty-three years ago on this very day, on this very spot, he lost his best friend. In this short account, he noted that while on this location they were separated, they were finally reunited by him returning. He also wanted his friend to know that he was not forgotten, that he still lived in his memory. He said to those gathered, "We want you to know Joe we still remember you."[51] On this fluid body of water, the ceremony included the placing of a memorial wreath. One veteran wrote of the meaning of returning with "a sacred vow was kept. The men of the Gambier Bay and VC-10, who sleep within her hull, can now rest in peace."[52]

For public historians, this demonstrates the lengths people will go to memorialize the dead and bring closure to past trauma, that to overcome the obstacle of memorializing on the ocean, to connect the present with the past, objects can in fact be invented. Manufactured decades later, a metal tube bridged thousands of feet of seawater, thirty years of life, and the survivors' need to find closure with an inaccessible and remote location.

Best Practices and Suggestions for Better Interpretation

- This Philippine pilgrimage showcases the inventive nature of naval commemoration for those sailors seeking closure with past wartime trauma.
- In fact, visiting the naval battlefield can be achieved to host a ceremony remembering those lost in a similar way to ceremonies remembering land battles.

Relics

Nearing the conclusion of World War II, the U.S. Navy edged closer and closer the Japanese homeland. In April 1945, the ever more desperate Japanese forces employed designed suicide attacks with aircraft in hopes of stunning the American enemy into some type of negotiated peace, preserving the emperor and the homelands from foreign invasion. On May 11, 1945, the Essex-class aircraft carrier the USS *Bunker Hill*, CV 17, was struck by two kamikazes. The resulting explosions, combined with the aircraft of CV 17 fully loaded with fuel and weapons on the flight deck, resulted in a conflagration that killed more than six hundred sailors. Due to the heroic efforts of the *Bunker Hill* sailors, she survived, and after extinguishing fires and draining water below decks that collected in battling fires, these exhausted sailors came to see the horror and the true cost of war. The recovery of the bodies was unbelievably difficult and it is hard to imagine what was worse, fellow sailors burned beyond recognition or those that died as a result of asphyxiation from blazing smoke and fumes concentrating pockets of poison gas below decks by the vessel's ventilation system. One of the sailors involved in this dreadful task made a discovery of some small objects, which he kept, and took the revelation of these items to his grave.

Dax Berg, a grandson of a USS *Bunker Hill* sailor, found an assortment of war memorabilia after the death of his grandfather. After the attack, Berg's grandfather, Robert Schock, found the charred remains of one of the two kamikaze pilots who had slammed into the vessel during the clean-up operation. Schock's discovery yielded a number of artifacts from the body, including a letter, a photo, a small piece of fabric from a life jacket, and a navigation watch worn around the neck, all of which Schock claimed and never told anyone about. The navigational watch was in amazing condition as the force of impact buried it inside the pilot's rib cage, which protected it from the explosion, a fact made clear with dried blood from its owner still on the surface.

Commemorating warfare as it moves forward in time from the original participants transforms. One of the metamorphoses that takes place is that the anger toward the enemy dissipates with each passing generation recalling the event. An example of this notion is the reaction of Dax Berg on finding the objects recovered from the kamikaze who struck his grandfather's carrier. He reached out to a reunion group of veterans in Japan composed around a kamikaze squadron.

Contacting the organization in Japan, Berg learned that the group consisted of mostly family members whose loved ones perished in carrying out kamikaze attacks. Berg reiterated his discovery of the objects his grandfather found on the unknown pilot from the USS *Bunker Hill*. Most relatives of the kamikaze pilots have no information on their family member as a result of no kamikaze pilots returning and reporting back on the successes or failures of the missions. During the war, they flew their missions and vanished. The piece of critical information on the identity of the pilot found by Schock, without him even knowing it, was the small piece of fabric, which on closer examination contained three letters of the pilot's name. This allowed the return of this collection of objects to the family members of Kiyoshi Ogawa.

The power of these objects, and the transference in meaning these possess for the next generation, is addressed by the historian Maxwell Taylor Kennedy in his book on the USS *Bunker Hill*. He wrote, "Many of the older Japanese especially feel a powerful connection to a person through his personal effects."[53] In the more traditional society of pre-war Japan, the objects of deceased family members could be assembled and maintained as a shrine to the love one. This is especially true of those lost in battle and whose remains were never recovered. Kennedy correctly notes that this notion is not so foreign from Western concepts in dealing with death. He wrote, "This is true also in Western societies, where we value the signature of a president or the clothing of a saint. These iconic mementos help us connect to an earlier time and make real the lives of distant people."[54]

The image returned by Burg showed four young Japanese pilots smiling in uniforms. There was also a handwritten letter dated just before Ogawa's final flight, the fragment of fabric with a portion of his name, and the watch used for navigation worn around his neck, fifty years after the war were returned to Japan. At some invisible point, human-invented gadgets can cross the line from inanimate object to relic. A simple manufactured watch, indecipherable from thousands of others, morphed into a relic for Ogawa's family. Knowing the timepiece survived the disintegration of the pilot and plane in a kamikaze attack by embedding inside Ogawa's body that he sacrificed for Japan sanctified this object. While an extreme example, Dax Berg's discovery, and more importantly his decision to return the objects, demonstrates the transformation that occurs for later generations after the shooting stops for any war.

Closing: "He Never Mentioned It to Me"

This chapter will end with another example of a naval relic returned to a family with the assistance of a reunion group. Such groups, beyond hosting reunions, act as conduits for those that possess and those that seek information on sailors who perished. Children of deceased veterans are a main source of inquiries as they pursue information on a loved one's service. Even decades after the death of the family member, they still thirst for better understand of their relatives. One such adult child, whose father died in 1974, inquired three decades after the death of his dad. He wrote, "[I] never had a chance to sit and talk with him about what he must have gone through. He never mentioned it to me."[55] In this unique role, reunions groups can fill the void for those born decades after the war seeking specific details on relatives.

One such individual was Annie McGillicuddy, who in 2004 contacted on organization about her uncle, Bill Roddy, who was killed on the USS *Barr* on May 29, 1944, in the same operation that claimed the USS *Block Island*. She discovered on the group's website a digital memorial listing all those killed on the USS *Barr*. She wrote, "Just visited your fine website. It is very moving to see my late Uncle's name, William A. Roddy."[56] She reported she know very little about him because "it was too painful for my parents to talk about and now the next generation is anxious to know about him."[57] The group provided information on the events of May 29 related to the USS *Barr* taking a torpedo while seeking to locate and destroy the cornered U-Boat. However, the group went another step further and placed a notice in their newsletter on this specific inquiry from a niece about the uncle she never knew.

Shipmate James "Ed" Ware contacted McGillicuddy and shared with her observations about Roddy he made in his wartime journal. This included that her uncle was a very religious person, and as a Catholic wore a medal of St. Christopher on his belt at all times. Over the course of correspondence, Ware shared more personal information on the death of Roddy. He related that after the aft portion of the USS *Barr* took a massive torpedo explosion, his thoughts went to those shipmates stationed there, including her uncle Roddy.[58] The explosion was horrific as the single torpedo strike detonated the USS *Barr*'s depth charges, which were placed there to drop on submerged U-Boats. Two men were mortally wounded and three other bodies were found; these five men were buried at sea the next day. However, the crew lost more than five men. The explosion was so violent it atomized twelve other sailors, leaving no trace.[59] Roddy was one of those that simply disappeared. However, Ware, in examining the smoldering wreckage in the vessel's aft, saw something small and familiar of Roddy's. He wrote, "It was here that I found the medal. The medal was tucked away following the war."[60]

Roddy's medal of St. Christopher underwent a number of transformations in meaning. For a Catholic like Roddy, it represented a religious pendant for protecting travelers. After the torpedo explosion that killed Roddy, once Ware found it and preserved it, the meaning certainly changed. For Ware, it could have represented his lost shipmates, the events of May 29, 1944, in the Atlantic, or the individual death of Roddy. Certainly Ware's meaning of the medal transformed in 2004 when he mailed it to McGillicuddy. As he wrote, "When I read about the niece of Bill's [Roddy] joining the USS Block Island Association, I wrote her and sent her the medal."[61]

Notes

1. Bill MacInnes, ed., *Chips Off the Old Block* 4 (1983): 10–12.

2. Kristin Ann Hass, *Carried to the Wall: American Memory and the Vietnam Veterans Memorial* (Berkeley: University of California Press, 1998), 2.

3. "Ship's Bells," Naval History and Heritage Command, http://www.history.navy.mil/faqs/faq83-1.htm (accessed May 18, 2011).

4. Ibid.

5. Robert M. Downie, "Block Island's Pair of Aircraft Carriers," *Providence Journal*, May 15, 1989, 12.

6. Ibid.

7. Shaun McKinnon, "'We Have to Remember': A Date Which Will Live in Infamy," *Arizona Republic*, December 7, 2015, 3A, 8A.

8. Dominick LaCapra, *History and Memory After Auschwitz* (Ithaca, NY: Cornell University Press, 1998), 9.

9. MacInnes, *Chips Off the Old Block* 3 (1986): 10–12.

10. MacInnes, *Chips Off the Old Block* 1 (1983): 1.

11. MacInnes, *Chips Off the Old Block* 3 (1985): 3.

12. James D. Hornfischer, *The Last Stand of the Tin Can Sailors: The Extraordinary World War II Story of the U.S. Navy's Finest Hour* (New York: Random House, 2004), 359.

13. Hector Vernetti, interviewed by Ben Hruska, December 12, 2010, Tempe, Arizona.

14. Ibid.

15. Object Number 06.05.2005, USS *Block Island* Collection, Block Island Historical Society, Block Island, Rhode Island.

16. "Top Secret Report on German Prisoners Taken Aboard the USS *Block Island*, CVE 21, January 14, 1944 From U-231," U.S. Navy, USS *Block Island* Association Collection, San Diego, CA, 1–6.

17. Ibid., 5.

18. Ibid., 6.

19. Fabio Gygi, "Shattered Experiences—Recycled Relics," in *Matters of Conflict: Material Culture, Memory and the First World War*, ed. Nicholas J. Saunders (New York: Routledge, 2004), 75.

20. Joseph A. Amato, *Rethinking Home: A Case for Writing Local History* (Berkeley: University of California Press, 2002), 4.

21. Object Number 06.10.2007, USS *Block Island* Collection, Block Island Historical Society, Block Island, Rhode Island.

22. Bill MacInnes, email message to the author, June 26, 2011.

23. Document Number 06.74.01, USS *Block Island* Collection, Block Island Historical Society, Block Island, Rhode Island.

24. Object Number 06.12.2007, USS *Block Island* Collection, Block Island Historical Society, Block Island, Rhode Island.

25. Letter to the BIHS from Ken Vachon, March 28, 2007, Block Island Historical Society, Block Island, Rhode Island.

26. Ibid.

27. Amato, *Rethinking Home*, 3.

28. Norman Polmar, *Aircraft Carriers: A Graphic History of Carrier Aviation and Its Influence on World Events* (Garden City, NY: Doubleday, 1969), 732.

29. Fletcher Pratt, *The Navy's War* (New York: Harper and Brothers, 1943), 184.

30. Ibid., 206.

31. Ibid.

32. "USS Franklin (CV 13) "The Ship That Wouldn't Die," USS *Franklin* (CV 13), http://www.ussfranklin.org (accessed November 14, 2011).

33. Ibid.

34. Alison Landsberg, *Prosthetic Memory: The Transformation of American Remembrance in the Age of Mass Culture* (New York: Columbia University Press, 2004), 129.

35. "The Big Ben Comes Home," *All Hands*, June 1945, Number 339, 20.

36. "USS Franklin (CV 13) The Ship That Wouldn't Die," USS *Franklin* (CV 13), http://www.ussfranklin.org (accessed November 14, 2011).

37. "The Big Ben Comes Home," 20.

38. "Exploring the Pharaoh's Boat," NOVA: Building Pharaoh's Ship, http://www.pbs.org/wgbh/nova/pharaoh/expl-nf.html (accessed December 10, 2015).

39. "Aurora: The Cruiser that Sparked a Revolution—Or Did It?" Russia Beyond the Headlines, http://rbth.com/arts/2014/11/07/aurora_the_cruiser_that_sparked_a_revolution_or_did_it_41229.html (accessed December 12, 2015).

40. Ibid.

41. "We Sank the Khukri," Pakistan Affairs, http://www.pakistanaffairs.pk/threads/9540-INS-Khukri-was-sunk-by-PNS-HANGOR-on-9-Dec-1971-41-yrs-back/page2 (accessed December 13, 2015).

42. "Karachi: Submarine Hangor on Display in Museum," Dawn, http://www.dawn.com/news/279766/karachi-submarine-hangor-on-display-in-museum (accessed December 13, 2015).

43. Ibid.

44. "Background," USS *Pueblo* (AGAR 2), http://www.usspueblo.org/index.html (accessed December 13, 2015).

45. "North Korea to Put US Spy Ship Captured in 1968 on Display," Guardian, http://www.theguardian.com/world/2013/jul/25/north-korea-us-spy-ship-museum (accessed December 13, 2015).

46. Stephen Pyne, *Voyager: Seeking Newer Worlds in the Third Great Age of Discovery* (New York: Viking Press, 2010), 166.

47. Samuel Eliot Morison, *History of United States Naval Operations in World War II Volume 12: Leyte, June 1944–January 1945* (Boston: Little, Brown, 1963), 275.

48. Tony Potochniak, *Return to the Philippines* (USS *Gambier Bay* Association, 2005), 1.

49. Ibid.

50. Ibid., 29.

51. Ibid.

52. Ibid., 35.

53. Maxwell Taylor Kennedy, *Danger's Hour: The Story of the USS Bunker Hill and the Kamikaze Pilot Who Crippled Her* (New York: Simon and Schuster, 2008), 457.

54. Ibid.

55. MacInnes, *Chips Off the Old Block* 1 (2006): 6.

56. MacInnes, *Chips Off the Old Block* 1 (2004): 2.

57. Ibid.

58. MacInnes, *Chips Off the Old Block* 3 (2006): 10.

59. Bill MacInnes, email to the author, June 12, 2011.

60. MacInnes, *Chips Off the Old Block* 3 (2006): 10.

61. Ibid.

CHAPTER 4

Exhibitions

PUBLIC HISTORIANS understand the relative data dump of war-related material the twentieth century offers compared to previous centuries. This fact is attested to with miles of paper documentation housed in government archives on just small aspects of World War II or the Vietnam War. Additionally, the civilian population's means of understanding World War II included new technological methods like radio broadcasts, numerous newspapers, and the showing of selected scenes of the war in movie theaters. After the war, these aspects of modernity shaping myth making greatly affected the recalling of World War II. The scholar Alison Landsberg addresses the impact of mass culture in transforming national understanding. According to her, "This new form of memory, which I call prosthetic memory, emerges at the interface between a person and a historical narrative about the past, at an experimental site such as a movie theater or museum."[1] Landsberg argues that central events from the American experience became critical aspects of citizens understanding themselves, even though just a handful of Americans experienced the event firsthand. She writes, "Through the technologies of mass culture, it became possible for these memories to be acquired by anyone, regardless of skin color, ethnic background, or biology."[2] Landsberg's suggestion, that transferability of memory can overcome the gap of experiencing an event firsthand, can also be applied to different generations of citizens. For example, mass culture holds the potential for transporting national understanding of World War II, and thus other historical events, to those that did not experience it. Thus, public historians in all fields possess a huge opportunity and responsibility in the construction and presentation of history. While Landsberg's theoretical construct of "prosthetic memory" may be too esoteric for the average museum visitor, or even the average museum profession, she points out a significant fact for those commemorating naval history.

Any consideration of exhibitions needs a brief examination of cultural memory. With regard to cultural memory and naval history, the scholars Suzanne Falgout, Lin Poyer, and Laurence M. Carucci, in their recent book *Memories of War: Micronesians in the Pacific War*, examine the means by which these indigenous inhabitants of Micronesia remember World War II. The group, composed of a diverse population encompassing a network of different languages in a range of Pacific islands, experienced the war with waves of both Japanese and American invasions. The authors note the complex practice of passing on this cultural history through oral traditions, dance, and songs to those who did not experience the war firsthand. As they wrote, "It is an ongoing process of social interaction and cultural creation through which people tell themselves, and others, stories about their past."[3] The authors emphasize the multifaceted nature of cultural memory in passing information on to future generations.

Moreover, the authors suggest the fragile nature of memory. They theorize this point by writing, "That is why we often hear the phrase 'lest we forget' and why we raise markers, observe anniversaries of important events, and engage in other memorial activities."[4] They agree with the scholar Pierre Nora when they note that if memory was not frail, sites of remembrance such as memorials and museums would not be needed. As Nora wrote, "We buttress our identities upon such bastions, but if what they defended were not threatened, there would be no need to build them."[5] The author's study, in drawing on the experience of the Micronesians, demonstrates the diversity of the ways in exhibiting the past in preserving naval memory for later generations. The need to remember is a part of being a member of any society. No matter the time, place, or people, inventing methods of remembering makes us human.

Battleship Cove

While reading most naval histories, authors sculpt text into scenes of action, of war vessels and their crews braving the high seas and the unseen enemy somewhere just over the horizon. However, at times over their working lives, war vessels are in fact stationary. That is, unexcitedly anchored off shore or securely fixed to a dock of knotted lines. Much like a star athlete requires food, rest, and shelter, so too for the fastest and toughest of vessels. Sea life is rough on men and machine no matter the century, and time at port allows for overhauling damaged sails and masts, refueling either in the form of coal, oil, or nuclear propulsion, and the transfer of sailors taking on new assignments. Also, in times of peace, vessels are shelved and placed in the mothball fleet. That is, with their usefulness over for the time being, ships are tethered to a buoy surrounded by other abandoned vessels with no activity on board other than the ocean's tide. For most vessels, this is nothing short of a death sentence. While some may be brought back into the fleet or converted into an auxiliary role, their working careers are winding down. The destiny of scrappage for most is certain; it is just a matter of time before cutting torches reduce used-up warships into future razor blades and automobile bumpers.

Today just a handful of World War II–era vessels remain. The main tactic employed by preservationists in saving retired warships is adaptive reuse. When a warship is decommissioned by a government, a historically minded organization will transform it into a museum piece. Morphing a moveable weapon of war into a stationary family-friendly environment is no easy feat. Exhibitions often take center stage, including displays of time-specific naval artifacts, or even radical structural overhaul of the vessel to include open space for a theater. Such ship-based organizations, located around the world, can be visited in New York, San Diego, and London. However, one ship-based organization in New England has just recently added a new exhibition that challenges past decades of curating. From the deck of a World War II–era battleship, visitors experience visual and audio components to exhibit and create a personal experience of the attack on Pearl Harbor. A battleship that survived the attack on Hawaii today acts as a stage for visitors in experiencing a recreated December 7, 1941, in Massachusetts.

Battleship Cove in Fall River, Massachusetts, has the largest floating tonnage of World War II–era vessels in the world with the battleship the USS *Massachusetts*, BB 59, destroyer the USS *Joseph P. Kennedy*, DD 850, and submarine the USS *Lionfish*, SS 298. For fifty years this museum, with the use of decommissioned U.S. Navy vessels, showcased and exhibited history on three geographic thematic levels, these being local, regional, and international. For example, Boy Scout groups spend the night on board a battleship and learn about life for young sailors from southern Massachusetts during World War II. On the regional level, the destroyer the USS *Joseph P. Kennedy* serves as a floating memorial to the older fallen brother of President John F. Kennedy, who died in the war. And finally, on the international level, these vessels' working careers highlight the global impact of the U.S. Navy on the twentieth century.

For five decades, Battleship Cove has been preserving and presenting naval history and just like the evolution in naval technology the methods employed by this museum entity also progressed overtime. Arguably, it's best known in the maritime museum community for leading the way in devising the first sleepover program on board the USS *Massachusetts*. In this, groups of Boy and Girl Scouts spend a full day on board the ship, including eating in the officer's mess and sleeping in bunks. The concept has been adopted by many other ship museums. In this vein, Battleship Cove has just opened an exhibition in which standing on the deck of a battleship visitors see a reenactment of the attack on Pearl Harbor.

One central theme of Battleship Cove is hands-on experience for visitors of all ages. As their promotional video to potential visitors states, it's "a museum where you get to climb, crawl, touch, and see it all." Every year since Lyndon Johnson was president, tens of thousands of visitors have immersed themselves in exploring the decks and galleys of a forty-thousand-ton vessel. However, with the upcoming seventy-fifth anniversary of the attack on Pearl Harbor, the curators sought a role reversal. Instead of the normal mode of the battleship housing exhibitions, the water in which she rests would function as a stage for the "Pearl Harbor Experience." Visitors stand on the deck and see a curator's attempt at recreating the attack that BB 59 survived that December morning. In concluding the advertisement, the museum promotes this new experience with "and that's not something you can get out of a history book."

With the use of surround sound, original footage projected on the outdoor screens, and submerged special effects simulating gunfire from Japanese planes, five times daily museum guests experience a recreation of the attack on Pearl Harbor from the vantage point of the USS *Massachusetts*, BB 59. As the museum states, "You will get to watch firsthand the attack on Pearl Harbor. Hear the roar of the planes, the whistle of the falling bombs, see water splashes of bullets and torpedoes." Using 4-D sound and archival filming of the actual attack, the immersion process creates for those with no point of reference of the attack in terms of living memory a foothold of understanding. As their executive director Brad King said in an interview, "We are introducing an exciting new experience seldom found within the museum world, connecting the audience with those men and women whose lives were permanently changed by the attack."[6]

This new exhibition from an old museum opens this chapter on naval exhibition. We as museum practitioners need to seek out such organizations with the unique combination of longstanding excellence in the field while also still retaining the passion to take chances and try new methods of historical interpretation. An additional reason to seek these models out is that every day twentieth-century history recedes further into the past. Meaning that with naval museums whose core area of preservation centers on World War II or the Cold War era, children on field trips will have no living memory of the twentieth century. Thus, producing exhibitions for visitors who experienced or who parents experienced an event is much different from those who have no personal connection to the era or conflict interpreted in exhibitions. Thus, Battleship Cove, in developing an exhibit on Pearl Harbor seventy-five years after the attack occurred, incorporated methods of sensory imagery to bring to life an event that for most children is just a date to remember for history exams, such as the year of the signing of the Declaration of Independence, the Apollo 11 moon landing, or the assassination of President Lincoln.

Best Practices and Suggestions for Better Interpretation

- Demonstrates inventive interpretation, that of a leader in the field of a ship-based World War II museum not afraid of tackling in a new direction of exhibition.
- Shows sensitivity to demographics of age, realizing that the static models of interpretation of the twentieth century will not connect with younger visitors.

La Belle, Bullock Museum

Off the coast of Texas, for years both amateur and professional divers sought the location of the shipwreck. In 1684, *La Belle*, part of a failed naval exposition launched by French king Louis XIV to establish a colony at the mouth of the Mississippi River, met disaster. She wrecked in Matagorda Bay in 1686 after a tremendous storm hit the area. The few crew that survived the ordeal at sea now faced another on land. For Texas history, the tale gravitated toward myth with no tangible evidence of the ill-fated voyage. However, after a twenty-year effort, in 1996 archaeologists diving finally located the wreck and a produced treasure trove for historians. A decades-long recovery effort of the 1.6 million objects, and a subsequent award-winning exhibition at the Bullock Museum of Texas History in Austin, exemplifies long-range planning, innovative design, and an exhibition reinforcing and at the same time redefining an institution's mission.

The recovery effort in short was nothing short of monumental. In the shallow waters on Matagorda Bay, a circular steel and copper dam was constructed and the saltwater pumped out. An archaeological dig spanning seven months followed; items recovered included cannons, glass beads, and rings.[7] More trade beads were uncovered on this wreck than all previous North American archaeological digs combined. The most challenging object, however, was what remained of *La Belle*. Succinctly, the expertise on safely recovering and implementing a successful preservation treatment for a submerged three-hundred-year-old wooden vessel did not exist. While pulling wooden objects out of the ocean was simple enough, doing it safely without the seventeenth-century wood rapidly deteriorating is a complex and time-consuming process.[8] Recovering, cataloging, and preservation efforts, however, represented just half the battle.

In developing "*La Belle*: The Ship That Changed History," the Bullock Texas State History Museum teamed up with Texas A&M University, the Texas Historical Commission, and, in France, the Musée National de la Marine. In this project/exhibition totaling some $10 million, the organization funding partners included the State of Texas, the National Endowment for the Humanities, the Institute for Museum and Library Services, and the Texas State History Museum Foundation.

Curatorial plans called for a permanent exhibition of eleven thousand square feet redefining the Bullock Museum and invited visitors into the production experience. Over a period of six months, guests were active observers in the layout and set up of the exhibition. While chaotic at times, inviting the public eye to see the piecing together of a large-scale exhibition was successful on two fronts. First, visitors learned that museum exhibitions are a complex and evolving processes. Second, in a world where more and more consumer products require short amounts of time, returning guests witnessed the dedication of staff in producing these quality productions.

As for the exhibition itself, the meticulously cleaned, cataloged, and preserved *La Belle* serves as the centerpiece.[9] As one curator said, "Something this large is very magnetic in a museum."[10] On the first floor of the Texas History Gallery, the ship is the main frame of reference in this exhibition reconsidering the early history of Texas and the United States. However, the ship does not overpower the exhibition. In demonstrating the intention of this French expedition to establish a new colony, the exhibition displays household objects such as a jug and colander. A bronze cannon gives visitors a glimpse of this as a military expedition as twenty-one thousand pounds of gunpowder found on board.[11]

Beside quality design and implementation, the exhibition demonstrates that history is an evolving process. Many people think history is just facts, which don't change, and if a public historian challenges this notion we run the risk of being branded with the dreaded term *revisionist*. The Bullock Museum director Dr. Victoria Ramirez speaks of the power of the singular discovery of *La Belle*. As she said, "The story itself introduces new scholarship in early

Texas history and the ship's hull and artifacts are in remarkable shape."[12] And to the point of challenging past versions, she states, "With each new discovery, history changes and *La Belle* has certainly made our understanding of the region more complete."[13]

While most of us in the field of naval history will never discover a shipwreck or assemble such a diverse group of international partners in an exhibition, lessons abound from this example. First, inviting the public eye into the exhibition development, while challenging, holds massive positive potential. Another is the use of a single centered object surrounded by thoughtfully placed secondary objects in telling a larger narrative. We can all consider the successful steps taken at the Bullock Museum.

> ## Best Practices and Suggestions for Better Interpretation
>
> - Prime example of how an exhibition can challenge visitors to review history on many levels including individual, regional, and national.
> - Demonstrates centering an exhibition with a single object—in this case the *La Belle*— which allows the exhibition goals to all stem from this single artifact.

Exhibitions and Kids

On the waterfront in New London, Connecticut, is the Custom House Museum devoted to the long maritime history of New London and Groton, where the Thames River enters the Long Island Sound. Located on Bank Street in a stone building constructed in 1833, a small room on the second floor still serves as a U.S. Custom Office, makes it the oldest active custom office in the United States. While exhibitions vary across themes and decades of naval history, one of the most successful is an exhibit devoted to children. The curator sheds light onto the nature of naval traditions onto U.S. society by showcasing toys used by American youth over 150 years ago.

In display cases, perceptively placed at lower levels for children standing or in strollers, but still visible from above by adults, are a collection of lead sailors. The differing numbers of sailors that vary in both individual figures and color schemes demonstrates the popularity of these toys at the time. A second case demonstrates how the naval theme penetrated beyond toys and into American youth culture with a box of Cracker Jack's from the early twentieth century, sporting a youth sailor in full uniform. Along this theme, comics and even a can of soda with the cartoon figure of Popeye the Sailor Man again demonstrate naval impact on early popular culture.

The exhibit carefully remembers to give a point of reference for youth visitors whose living memory extends only a decade or two, and incorporates modern naval-themed toys such as Bart Simpson in a pirate outfit and assemblages of Legos into naval vessels. Lastly, an additional display case highlights naval-themed American youth fashion outfits modeled after sailors' uniforms that include caps.[14] This children's exhibit brings balance with traditional and nontraditional components and demonstrates a museum considering visitors of all ages.

Figure 4.1. A lead sailor on display at a children's exhibit at the New London Custom House Maritime Museum. Photo by Ben Hruska.

Incorporating a well-designed section to engage kids is very a sound practice. In terms of naval history, the Customs House Museum designed and wonderfully provides a top-notch example for us to consider naval themes and younger visitors.

A Question of Scale: Patriot's Point

Utilizing the term *platform of memory*, this work argues that the transformation of World War II–era naval vessels into exhibition space holds the potential for shaping visitors' understanding of the U.S. Navy, aviation history, and American wars. The majority of World War II vessels that serve as modern-day platforms of memory served after the war for decades. Thus, the narrative of the vessel's individual history is much more than just World War II. Exhibition space also encompasses the other operations conducted from the ship and the other generations of American sailors who served on board in the Cold War. In this modern form of visiting a singular place, that of a ship, to experience firsthand a World War II carrier, visitors also learn much more than just this single vessel's role in the war. These also tell the story of the greater role of the U.S. Navy, classification of other naval vessels that did not survive, and technological innovations effecting carriers and aircraft in the second half of the twentieth century.

The decade of the 1970s in the United States was one of identity. The nation itself celebrated its two hundredth birthday and also sought national meaning in healing from the multitude of questions stemming from the violence of the 1960s. Assassinations, riots, the war in Vietnam, and Watergate all required national reexamination of itself and a search for bearings to make sense of a decade of chaos. Thus, in the 1970s, museums, monuments, and genealogical societies increased exponentially.

In 1975, a group mostly composed of retired U.S. Navy sailors, some with thirty years of service and some with just a few, started a pioneering voyage in naval preservation and interpretation. Their mission, transforming the Essex-class aircraft carrier the USS *Yorktown*, CV 10, designed as a mobile platform of warfare for young sailors into a stationary museum attraction for visitors of all ages, backgrounds, and physical abilities, was monumental. While turning a vessel of war into a museum was nothing new, doing so for a vessel that held nearly three thousand sailors, that could maintain and store ninety aircraft, and displaced over thirty-five thousand tons, had not.[15] Like the transforming mission of a ship, so too would the evolution of interpreting naval history for forty years at Patriot's Point Naval and Maritime Museum reshape the harbor of Charleston, South Carolina.

The preservation of a human-engineered structure by morphing its mission is not unique to naval history, as seen in small local historical museums housed in former schools, railroad depots, places of worship, and courthouses. In any transformation questions arise, such as: What should remain to serve as a testament to the original function of the structure? What should be transformed in this "old" structure to accommodate the new influx of museum visitors? As David Clark, a founding member of the *Yorktown* staff, wrote, "We had no professional museum/exhibit expertise present to help in the 'grey area' of what spaces aboard ship were expendable for exhibits."[16] Some choices centered on visitor safety, and in the design of passageways in an exhibition space, cutting torches were employed in removing hatch doors all the way to the floors, thus removing the previously needed compartmentalized room required of a ship at sea.

They also faced the question that all museum professionals of long-servicing vessels face: namely, what time period should be interpreted? For example, the *Yorktown* served in the last two years of World War II; however, in the 1950s she received a major "facelift" that included modification to launch and maintain jet fighters. Additionally, all communication and technological equipment on board date from the 1960s. Would the vessel be displayed as a World War II–era carrier waging war in the Pacific, a 1950s carrier in the Cold War, or 1960s carrier used in retrieving members of Apollo 8 who parachuted safely to the ocean's surface?

In the opening years, maintenance swallowed the majority of staff and volunteer hours on this vast vessel, which had been exposed to thirty years of seawater and salt air. As Clark noted, "A capital warship [aircraft carrier or battleship] in commission has a large work force available for routine maintenance." This ship that survived the scrapyards, after a lifetime of service, would have less than 1 percent of this work force.[17] Of the *Yorktown* in this early phase, Clark wrote, "Every chance I had back then I would explore the uncharted areas of *Yorktown*. There were many cat walks I was afraid to walk on, peeling paint, etc."[18]

Because so much effort was diverted by early staff to making the vessel safe, the exhibitions were left up to volunteer organizations. Veterans groups such as local American Legion Posts, and veterans from certain carriers such as the *Saratoga* and the *Monterey*, produced and installed exhibitions. These exhibitions, spanning from 1977 to 1995, with their own themes and curating goals, resulted in overlapping and an overall disjointed interpretative narrative. However, with the fiftieth anniversary of World War II, Patriot's Point harnessed the funding needed for an overhauling of the exhibition space with professional museum employees, including an in-house professional graphic shop, improved construction of exhibits, and incorporating well-designed educational components.

The shift in taking over the interpretation from volunteer organizations was a key to the success at Patriot's Point. This statement is not taking a shot at volunteer-based projects, as we will later examine an award-winning exhibition produced by an all-volunteer organization with no paid employees. Rather, the *Yorktown* was confronted by not a volunteer problem, but also numerous exhibitions completed by different groups over a number of years. Thus, overlap and no single central curatorial theme were the main problems that surfaced. This conversion to exhibits from a single producer of imagination has been near total. Not only has the *Yorktown*'s exhibitions and educational programs coalesced around a central mission, it has expanded onto the four-hundred-acre location on Charleston Harbor deeded to the organization by the South Carolina General Assembly. Thus, today the site includes a memorial to the Cold War, the Medal of Honor Museum, and the Vietnam Experience Exhibit. Additionally, the submarine the USS *Clamagore*, SS 343, and the destroyer the USS *Laffey*, DD 724, are also preserved and on display.[19] However, with all these large-scale successes, it is important to note one failure, which is common in all aspects of the museum world and especially for ship-based organizations.

This is not to demonstrate a weakness in leadership at the site, but to note that even the most successful institutions at time confront failure. The organization accepted into the collection a rather unique vessel and devised ambitious plans calling for the ship to serve as both exhibition space and facilities for a hotel and restaurant. The overall goal germinated in seeing a similar model of success with the *Queen Mary* located in Long Beach, California. If successful, visitors could spend more than just a few hours at Patriot's Point. The vessel, the N.S. *Savannah*, was part of President Eisenhower's Atoms of Peace program and was the world's first nuclear-powered merchant ship. With funding and manpower already spread thin, the project stalled. After several years, the U.S. Maritime Administration dry docked the *Savannah*; after reporting back, the decision was made to pass on continuing the effort.[20]

The decision for any museum to take on a decommissioned ship in order to save it is much easier than accepting it in your collection, developing a curatorial plan, and raising the required funds. Remember the adage about new watercraft: "A boat is a hole in the water into which you pour money." Then think of decades of seawater and rust, environmental concerns such as lead paint and asbestos insulation on piping, on top of the work in converting ship spaces into exhibition and educational areas. While it is easy to see the triumphs in naval preservation, it is important to know that even the most successful organizations struggle with what to take on and what ship projects should not be attempted.

Pima Air and Space Museum

In Tucson, Arizona, is the Pima Air and Space Museum, adjacent to the Davis-Monthan Air Force Base. Housing over two hundred historic air and spacecraft, the Pima Air Museum viewed from the highway in a passing vehicle could be mistaken for the aviation equivalent of a "building zoo." This term refers to an assemblage of historic buildings that retain no historic connection, thrust together by happenstance as the result of these structures surviving demolition in various locations and compiled to recreate a time period from the past. While the application of this term at Pima could be applied to the display with rows of differing aircraft outside, five aircraft hangars include well-planned exhibitions. Exhibitions cover a vast spectrum of aviation history; however, two naval topics deserve consideration.

Freshwater Aircraft Carriers

Great exhibits inform by challenging visitors. In the hangar devoted to World War II is one aircraft of which thousands were built, yet the province of this fighter aircraft is truly unique and the condition of it on display grants a window that disputes popular interpretations of the U.S. Navy. The General Motors FM-2 (F4F) Wildcat first stands out in the hangar filled with impeccably restored aircraft, as the original painting, being sixty years old, is cracked and faded. Just the nose of the Wildcat has been restored to the dark blue hue, adding further distinction to the Wildcat. Attracted visitors read the exhibit display and learn that this aircraft was submerged for fifty years in Lake Michigan near Chicago. Understanding what the aircraft endured, visitors are surprised at how good a shape it is in. Lost as the result of a naval aviator learning to take off and land on the deck of an aircraft carrier, this exhibit, centered with the Wildcat, introduces visitors to the U.S. Navy's "Freshwater Aircraft Carriers."

A large display case personalizes the recovered aircraft with objects found in the cockpit. An oxygen regulator, a navigation plotting wheel, and the pilot's hankie all shed light on the young naval aviator learning the very complex operation of taking off and landing on a moving flight deck. Next to these objects is a model of one of the two freshwater aircraft carriers. The USS *Sable*, IX-81, and the USS *Wolverine*, IX-64, were of the same side wheel–powered design, and both were originally constructed to ferry passengers on the Great Lakes. Constructed in the early part of the twentieth century, the *Seeandbee* and the *Greater Buffalo*, once converted during the war, completed training for carrier operations in the middle of the country completely removed from any enemy submarine activities. They had no hangar deck for storing and repairing aircraft, no living quarters for hundreds of sailors below, just a five-hundred-foot-long wooden flight deck that could cruise off Chicago at eighteen knots. Over the course of the war, some eighteen thousand pilots logged an estimated 116,000 takeoffs and landings. Due to these being the young pilot's first five, these operations proved dangerous to men and machines, and accidents results in numerous aircraft being lost, including this General Motors FM-2 Wildcat with serial number 16161.

The unique factors of Lake Michigan, including the depth, cold temperature, and freshwater, resulted in just a fraction of the deterioration caused by saltwater. A chemistry lesson in the differences between salt and freshwater is visually seen with the Wildcat on display. While the repainted nose of the craft at first highlights the deterioration, once the viewer realizes it was submerged for over half a century in Lake Michigan, the inverse perspective takes hold.[21] Ten presidents had been elected and taken the oath of office since this FM-2 fighter crashed during a training operation from the aircraft carrier. The unique discovery, interpreted with an equally unique exhibition, informs visitors on the U.S. Navy's Great Lake freshwater aircraft carriers. This task is completed with informational text, images, and objects. The imperfect Wildcat, standing apart from the other aircraft in the hangar, first draws the viewer in, interpretative text testifies to the rich naval history of Chicago and the freshwater carriers, and lastly small objects pulled from the cockpit give a human element. The static plane, combined with a surviving hankie and oxygen regulator, comes to life as an airplane someone was utilizing in training for war, and during that training crashed into the water.

Nose Art and Insignia: Beyond the Girls

Across the hangar from the Wildcat pulled out of the cold dark waters of Lake Michigan is an exhibition not using fully restored planes, but just small portions of the fuselage. Hanging

Figure 4.2. A Wildcat fighter on display at the Pima Air and Space Museum, which was pulled out of Lake Michigan after being submerged for fifty years. Photo by Ben Hruska.

on the hangar wall are portions of former aircraft, most just two to three feet in height and width. On each of the metal surfaces, painted over seams and series of linear and horizontal rivets, rests nose art in a vast array of designs, color arrangements, and imagery of humans and animals. A short and insightful text section away from the wall interprets the meaning of these works of art that gained fame in the First World War. Nose art can be organized into two groupings: official and unofficial. Of the former, the exhibits text states, "The official insignia are intended to raise morale and provide a sense of community and identity for the units whose aircraft display them."[22] Of the latter, the curator wrote, "The much more personal 'nose art' expressed the wants, fears, and hopes of the crews."[23]

With just one panel for text and approximately twenty-five sections of fuselage displaying nose art and insignia, this exhibition proves true the old Western adage "it's not how you rig up, it's how you ride." In a prime aviation museum with over two hundred examples of aircraft, this simple exhibition personifies not only these small pieces of metal, but also the surrounding restored aircraft. Young men went off to serve their nation full of many emotions, and in the compartmentalized and regimented existence of the military were allowed few visual outlets for self- and group expression. This small exhibit space not only completes the curator's design objective, but mirrors a tiny component in a much larger machine and functions in bringing a much-needed human context to the large testaments to aviation at the Pima Air and Space Museum.

Best Practices and Suggestions for Better Interpretation

- Both examples at the Pima Air and Space Museum incorporate making human connections to objects, thus avoiding the trap of interpretation redundancy many large artifact-based museums can easily fall into.
- Exhibits demonstrate that interpretation can take place without a completely restored aircraft, as in the examples of the plane fished out of Lake Michigan or just the small portions of fuselage.

Platform of Memory

The historian Shameem Black, in writing of commemorating the Holocaust, composed a simple but poignant sentence. She wrote, "To commemorate is not the same as to remember."[24] Commemoration involves action, organization, and some form of trust. Ship-based museums, in morphing from a platform for weapons to one of preserving and protecting history, undergo evolving missions and tactics. Similar to evolving naval strategy, institutions such as ship-based museums also transform over time in serving as harbors for naval history. For large World War II–era carriers that morphed into museums, these collect, gather, and display artifacts outside of their individual vessels. Their mission is greater than themselves, for these can be expanded and embrace the greater history of the U.S. Navy, World War II, the Cold War, or man's exploration of space. As a result, individual naval veterans entrust museums as a place to preserve and exhibit artifacts related to their wartime experiences. Such donations increase exponentially as veterans near the end of their lives.

Of the over seventy-five smaller escort carriers (CVEs) that served in the U.S. Navy, none survived to serve as a memorial. However, veterans of these ships improvised and located other carrier museums as a platform of remembrance. With escort carrier reunion groups lobbying with the large CV-based museums, three organizations agreed to devote exhibition space specifically for the history of the escort carriers, and once given this space, reunion groups announced to their membership the need for artifacts.[25] On the website of the Escort Carrier Sailors and Airmen Association (ESCAA), items were requested that included ship's newspapers, flight suits, hammocks, cups, and silverware. As the site pleaded, "These ships have set aside compartments in which only CVE displays and memorabilia will be exhibited."[26] The empowerment these veterans felt with this space in which to tell their own story was clearly evident. It continued, "Our 'museums' on these ships will be visited by millions of people each year, and it is up to us to send these museums our 'stuff' to display."[27]

Instead of these objects from the war remaining with the individual veterans, or with their families after their deaths, this group sought to incorporate these objects in exhibitions on the greater history of the U.S. Navy. While a core mission of these platforms of memory was to commemorate the individual history of a particular fast fleet carrier through exhibition, other stories were also told. Like these massive ships during the war hosting a range of compartmentalized functions for baking bread, working on planes, and housing the sailors, so too were former war vessels at museums home to multiple exhibition tasks taking place simultaneously.

Constructing Memorials

The anthropologist Nicholas J. Saunders, in his study of memory and World War I, wrote of the holistic approach individual veterans employed in dealing with wartime trauma. Utilizing objects from the war, such as shells, bullets, and uniforms, veterans constructed memorials to their individual pain and to lost comrades. Some of these homemade objects required constant attention, such as memorials made of brass shells, which quickly tarnished. Saunders paid attention to this fact of the ritual of cleaning the brass. He wrote, "Perhaps reinforced by the sensory dimension of the smell of brass polish, cleaning these objects may have been transformed from a banal chore to a sacred act, bridging the gap between the living and the dead."[28] The hours spent in constructing and maintaining these private memorials provided veterans an outlet for dealing with their wartime experiences.

For naval veterans, the construction of personal memorials held the potential for bridging the gap between their maritime service and their postwar lives. For example, once out of the service and residing on land, building models of their ships not only served as a reminder of their naval experience, but also aided in producing a nonverbal summation of their past life for those closest to them. The models provided a window into their individual experience. A discerning eye is needed to see the memorial, as a plastic model at first glance can easily be construed as just a toy. If constructed by a child, these would in fact be toys in terms of meaning; however, for naval veterans, the symbolic significance is much deeper and more complex. For example, veterans with the use of handmade models can recall their survival of a sinking.

A reduction in scale of a vessel from one of tens of thousands of tons to one of small plastic pieces does not equate to a reduction of meaning. For many, their entire wartime experience on board, shipmates, battles, and wartime experience is reduced to a few ounces of plastic. If framed and used properly, exhibitions can harness this interpretative power of ship models.

Joe Macchia served on the escort carrier the USS *Card*, CVE 11. His involvement in the commemoration of his ship is extensive, as he organized the first reunion for the USS *Card* crewmembers. In speaking of ways of remembering his service, he first talked about building a model.[29] A model company in the 1980s issued a 1/700 scale of the escort carrier the USS *Bogue*, CVE 9. This particular ship was one of eleven of the Bogue class and represented the first series of escort carriers. The veterans who served on any of these vessels can reconstruct their wartime ship with each model including a superstructure, flight deck, and individual aircraft. The model builder, given a great deal of control, has the power to select which number to place on the hull to coincide with their individual vessel. Builders also choose the number of planes on the flight deck and paint schemes for the hull. Resting on shelves and bookcases in sailors' homes, these serve as a visual testament in storytelling, a silent yet vehement symbol of naval service decades ago. Any visit to an American Legion hall will almost certainly demonstrate the symbolic power of naval models with members constructing and donating visual memorials to their vessels. The one major irony of this self-memorial construction by individual crewmembers of escort carriers was the company, Tamiya of Japan, which manufactured the model kit.[30] While crewmembers could spend hours piecing together a testament to past service, the plastic components making up the memorial were molded in Japan.

The symbolic power of vessels for naval veterans is not a new phenomenon. For millennia, those cultures that retained strong connections to maritime exploration and trade utilized ships as symbolic metaphors. As the archeologist Chris Ballard wrote, "Representations of boats appear in rituals associated with transitions in the lives of individuals, such as initiation, marriage, and death."[31] In his comparative study in examining the rock art of the maritime cultures of the Scandinavian and Southeast Asian Bronze Ages, Ballard argues that the symbolic power of ships was manifold. He writes that a ship was the "expression(s) of corporate identity and communal unity, and a critical symbol in rituals that mark major transitions in the lifecycle."[32] Depictions of ships in rock art held symbolic power denoting major events that called for preservation, a need that transcended both regions of the world and centuries of time. In recent centuries, naval veterans harnessed this long tradition of preservation and artwork, and thus maintained their wartime experiences for future remembrance.

On October 25, 1944, the USS *St. Lo*, CVE 63, took a direct hit from a bomb-loaded kamikaze. The impact into the flight deck ignited a fire that initiated further explosions and secondary fires that claimed the life of the vessel.[33] The USS *St. Lo* veterans started the process of holding reunions in the early 1980s.[34] In seeking to construct a testament to their lost ship and crewmembers, the board of directors of the USS *St. Lo* Association voted for an investigation into the production of a painting at their 1989 annual meeting. A commission was given to the naval artist Richard C. Moore, who completed the artwork by the time of the 1990 annual meeting. Moore had personal contact with forty people who experienced the kamikaze attack and subsequent sinking. He titled his work "The End of a Fighting Ship: The Last Moments of the USS St. Lo."[35] The work showed the CVE with black smoke billowing into a Pacific sky. While men are seen sliding down lines on the bow, an explosion is engulfing the aft portion of the ship. A testament not only to the crewmen and vessel lost, this painting also testifies to the bravery of the veterans who survived this trial.

For survivors, this artwork showing the demise of their ship communicated the near incommunicable experience. Like the rock art from centuries before, it also symbolized lifecycles. It functioned in marking into the historical record the fighting death of both the ship and the men who died defending her in the Battle of Samar. However, the selection for the display of the piece of art also needs consideration. The painting depicting the fighting death of the *St. Lo* was donated to the National Museum of Naval Aviation located in Pensacola, Florida.[36] This gift of art demonstrates veterans' tactics in seeking to save their ship and experience from the oblivion of forgotten actions of mankind. An institution dedicated to preserving the greater scope of U.S. naval aviation retains and preserves this testament to their loss. Collectively, the veterans of CVE 63 produced a visual testament to their sinking and then located an institution to house it into perpetuity.

Nuclear-Powered Exhibit

For the U.S. Navy, the naming of aircraft carriers has changed over time. From the commissioning of the first carrier in 1922 until the end of World War II, these vessels for the most part were named after famed battles from American history or past vessels within the navy. For example, during World War II the USS *Bunker Hill*, CV 17, and the USS *Yorktown*, CV 5, achieved fame in the Pacific war and were read about by the American public in daily newspapers. However, after the war, in October 1945, a carrier was named after the late president, the USS *Franklin D. Roosevelt*, CVB 42. After this event most names returned to those of famed ships or battles. But with the launch of the first nuclear-powered aircraft carrier, the Nimitz classification (CVN) in 1972, all names centered on individuals. The first was Admiral Nimitz; the classification of CVN was not only named after him, but the first vessel of the series also became the USS *Nimitz*, CVN 68. Of the other nine commissioned in this series, two were named for members of Congress and the remaining seven after presidents. Beyond retaining just the name, these vessels take on facets related to the president. For example, the USS *Theodore Roosevelt*, CVN 71, is called "America's Big Stick," and on the USS *Harry S. Truman*, CVN 75, one sees the adage "Give 'Em Hell."[37] However, on board the cavernous hangar decks of said vessels is also exhibition space.

Walking on board the USS *Theodore Roosevelt*, CVN 71, and into the hangar deck with space to hold up to sixty aircraft one is surrounded by history. On the white walls, in deep blue cursive, are the initials T. R. In the middle of the hangar deck, in the main passageway for crewmembers to exit and enter, is a massive glass display case. Inside is the taxidermied head of a bull moose, noting Theodore Roosevelt's running for the presidency in 1912 on a third party's ticket, the Progressive "Bull Moose" party. Above the moose is the title "'Bully' the Moose and Theodore Roosevelt." Surrounding the mount are images not only of Roosevelt as a hunter, but also staccato photographs pointing to his legacy as a preservationist with the creation of the modern National Park Service and placement of more than

Figure 4.3. A mural merging naval history and Harry S. Truman on display in the hangar deck of the USS *Harry S. Truman*, CVN 75. Photo by Ben Hruska.

200 million acres under the protection of various federal government agencies. But the display of history is well beyond just this small exhibition space on this ninety-three-thousand-ton vessel. On the flight deck are open-topped vehicles, very small in size and possessing tremendous torque in shuttling aircraft. The sides have "Aircraft Intermediate Maintenance Department" painted in white in a circular formation. Inset inside this circle is a painted picture of Roosevelt sporting his pince-nez spectacles. Looking up at the bridge of the vessel painted in red, white, and blue against the battleship gray is the ship's motto "Welcome to America's Big Stick."[38] This of course stems from the African proverb spoken by Roosevelt, "Speak softly and carry a big stick."

This trend of naming these new nuclear-powered carriers after presidents is not going away. The years 2003 and 2009 saw the commissioning of carriers named for Ronald Reagan and George H. W. Bush. Additionally, the year 2016 will see the first commissioning of the new series of carriers named after naval veteran and president Gerald R. Ford, and the first of this series will be named after him as well. The second carrier of the series will be named for President John F. Kennedy. These vessels, costing $4 billion and with a projected service life of fifty years, will be exhibiting the history of these two presidents who were also World War II naval veterans.[39]

Figure 4.4. The twenty-sixth president is exhibited throughout the Nimitz class nuclear-powered aircraft carrier the USS *Theodore Roosevelt*, CVN 71. Photo by Ben Hruska.

The Spanish-American War

America's shortest war was arguable its most popular war. The Spanish-American War lasted just 113 days, sold piles of print newspapers covering the fast-paced events in Cuba and the Philippines, and launched the political career of the leader of the Rough Riders, Lieutenant Colonel Theodore Roosevelt. For the United States, winning a war against a European power in the West Indies and in the Pacific was a huge victory with less than four hundred men killed in combat, and around two thousand perishing of wounds and disease. Despite the United States acquiring Puerto Rico and Cuba, the stunning victory of Admiral George Dewey over the Spanish fleet at the Battle of Manila Bay was the most startling development of the war.[40] The year 1898 marked the rapid rise of the U.S. Navy's reputation, which would only increase with Theodore Roosevelt becoming president.

Beyond America's first full venture in imperialism, the major societal impact of the brief war was the nation healing from the Civil War. As the historian Dale L. Walker writes, "Thirty years had passed since the tumult of the Civil War, time to ponder our place in the scheme of things, time to look outward to detect our Manifest Destiny, as we had in the great expansionist era of the 1840s."[41] A generation removed from Gettysburg and Petersburg, the next cycle of young men, both from the North and the South, took up arms together. This theme of reconciliation continued in the decades after the war in public exhibitions.

On the campus of the University of Tampa is an object on public exhibition. A gun installed at Fort Dade in 1898 for the defense of Tampa was selected as a public memorial for the Spanish-American War. Gifted and erected in 1927, the gun points south toward Cuba and the direction of the war. The large cement base, painted white, is framed with sections of black lettering providing context on the conflict and this public exhibition, including information on the committee and veterans group behind the formation of the marker.

Erected nearly thirty years after the war, the other sides of the cement note other portions of the war, including naval aspects. One panel utilizes local history and informs readers that this very spot, which today is so close to departing cruise ships, was the headquarters of Theodore Roosevelt's Rough Riders in their time in Tampa before departing for Cuba. Another panel holds the only human face, an inset motif, of Admiral George Dewey, below which text marks his May 1, 1898, victory at Manila Bay. The battleship the USS *Maine*, which exploded under mysterious circumstances on February 15, 1898, and sparked tensions that led to the war, is remembered with an inset wreath. Below this is the slogan from the period, "Remember the Maine." Lastly, this public exhibition marks reconciliation of the Civil War. On the base reads, "This war brought the blue of the cold bleak north and the gray of the sunny south into one great brotherhood and liberty to an oppressed people."

This public marker is unique and worth examining for a number of reasons beyond the light it sheds on a nearly forgotten conflict. In stands out being on a university campus; while campuses hold many different forms of war memorials, these normally are devoted to soldiers or sailors who were students at the college either before or after the war in question. This naval gun as a centerpiece marks the spot of military encampment, which was later taken over by the University of Tampa. Second, with such a short duration of the conflict, the public memorial marks military aspects of the U.S. Army, such as the first U.S. volunteer cavalry regiment, and naval components of the war such as the loss of the USS *Maine* and the hero status of Admiral Dewey. Additionally, this example demonstrates the use of an old and outdated naval cannon not only in marking a victory and commemorating a conflict, but also in attempt to heal a divided nation still grappling with the division of a Civil War that cost the lives of over six hundred thousand Americans. This public exhibition takes an ecumenical approach in memorials, embracing a specific place connected to the war and placing a marker to both the army and navy while seeking to ease the wounds from an earlier conflict that pitted a nation against itself.

John Paul Jones

The mortal remains of John Paul Jones rest in the crypt beneath the Chapel of the United States Naval Academy in Annapolis, Maryland. Born in Scotland and first learning seamanship on the high seas in the British Royal Navy, John Paul Jones gained fame as a marauder during the American Revolution. As the nascent American Navy could in no way take on the largest naval power in the world, Jones had success raiding vulnerable British ships isolated from the grand fleets of the empire. Additionally, beyond sea victories, the exploits of John Paul Jones boosted American morale in the long conflict full of many setbacks. For these accomplishments, John Paul Jones is sometimes considered the "Father of the American Navy."

The tomb is composed of a large black marble sarcophagus atop four carved dolphins and is guarded by a U.S. Marine sentry standing watch in the crypt. Against the circular crypt walls, displayed in cases and on wall space, is the documentation of Jones's receivership of his commissioning in the U.S. Navy, reproductions of his medals, and artwork depicting the naval hero. All objects on display in the crypt point to the foundational impact of Jones's service in the very early days of American naval history. Thus, visitors seeing the pageantry celebrating John Paul Jones's career on display would probably be surprised that he was laid to rest at the Naval Academy Chapel 114 years after his death.[42] Previous to being guarded by a Marine sentry, his grave rested unmarked in Paris. An examination into John Paul Jones's morphing from forgotten hero into the center of attention in a grand funeral a century after his death provides a unique window into the notion of a state funeral serving as an exhibition interpreting naval history.

After the American Revolution, John Paul Jones moved on to Russia and served in its Imperial Navy. He considered himself a "citizen of the world," and after his relationship with the Russia Imperial Court deteriorated, he lived in revolutionary France. It was here in 1792 that Jones died essentially unnoticed. Just a few loyal friends and officials buried him in a graveyard for foreign Protestants. In the decades that followed, the cemetery experienced neglect and transformed into a vegetable garden, a site for dog and cock fighting, and a dumping ground for dead animals. In the first years of the twentieth century, the American ambassador to France became interested in finding his grave. In a multiyear effort involving $35,000 in government funds authorized by the U.S. Congress and the naval enthusiast President Theodore Roosevelt, the employment of Parisian labors in digging tunnels under the site found a lead-lined coffin containing Jones.

Extracted from the ground beneath a site of ill repute, the pomp and circumstance commenced. With the American flag draped over his coffin, Jones's body paraded down crowded Paris streets on the way to Cherbourg. Here, boarding the USS *Brooklyn*, the body was escorted across the Atlantic by a fleet of eleven French and American vessels. Several cities, including Philadelphia, Washington, D.C., and Annapolis requested his body, however the U.S. Naval Academy won the honor and a year later a grand funeral served as an exhibition on Jones's career and also a potent symbol for a young president seeking an expanded U.S. Navy.

On April 24, 1906, to a gathered crowd of a thousand, Theodore Roosevelt stood on a ten-foot-high platform and projected his voice. Displayed both around the speaking platform and on the ceiling above Roosevelt, bunting of the stars and stripes set the tone for this memorial service. On the floor of the chapel in front of the president and the gathered crowd was the flag-draped coffin of John Paul Jones.[43] Roosevelt spoke of the outpouring of locations offering their site as the place of burial. He stated, "But I feel that the place of all others in which the memory of the dead hero will most surely be a living force is here in Annapolis."[44] This "living force" of John Paul Jones he reiterated throughout the speech.

In a public eulogy of this naval hero who died a century before this, the president interpreted Jones's service and how it was applicable to the modern listener and the modern U.S. Navy.

To be fair to Roosevelt, and not simply portray him as a politician using a eulogy as a platform for political gain, naval history was something dear to his heart. He was a naval historian. As a young man and just one year out of Harvard, he published his first book, *The Naval War of 1812*. He served as assistant secretary of the navy before the Spanish-American War, and with the outbreak of the war, he resigned his position to serve in the first United States volunteer cavalry, popularly known as the Rough Riders. Simply put, when he became president in 1901 after the assassination of President William McKinley, the navy had never had a better ally in the White House. He expanded the number of ships and sent what became known as the Great White Fleet around the world in a demonstration of American power. He encouraged and supported a revolution in Panama, which at the time was a part of Colombia, allowing the construction of the Panama Canal. And lesser known, he supported the allocation of $35,000 of funds in the location of John Paul Jones's body from a pauper's grave.[45] As a student of history and a man who would write over thirty books in his lifetime, Roosevelt understood the power of public symbols to embody complex themes. The career of John Paul Jones would serve as a vessel for Roosevelt lobbying for preparedness through the means of a strong navy.

Roosevelt, in speaking on the grounds of the academy, kept invoking or exhibiting the career of John Paul Jones. To the thousand people in attendance he said, "Moreover, the future naval officers, who live within these walls, will find a career of the man whose life we this day celebrate, not merely a subject for admiration and respect, but an object lesson to be taken into their innermost hearts."[46] This "object lesson" of Jones's life, that of courage in taking on the strongest naval force on the planet, Roosevelt reiterated was only half the requirement for a modern navy in the first decade of the twentieth century. As naval warfare had evolved with increasingly complicated ships of war, tactics, and technologies, preparedness was essential. With modernity, the days of taking to the sea for battle without careful planning or cultivation of naval officers were over. Thus, he exhibited Jones's career in the importance of merging courage and readiness. As the leading advocate of a strong navy, in the conclusion of his eulogy, Roosevelt stated, "Remember that no courage ever atones for lack of that preparedness which makes courage valuable."[47]

In obtaining a strong navy, Roosevelt did everything in his constitutional authority to achieve these ends. Nudging a revolution in Colombia, constructing the Panama Canal, and sending a fleet around the world all assisted in reaching his lofty goal of creating the strongest navy in the world. Additionally, understanding the power of symbols, he funded the effort to find the body of John Paul Jones, gave his eulogy, and selected the location of his grave to exhibit the man considered the "Father of the American Navy."

The National Museum of the Pacific War

World War II veterans and family members seeking to remember their ship and crewmembers could select the tactic of the dedication of a memorial plaque at the National Museum of the Pacific War. Located in Fredericksburg, Texas, the museum was founded at the boyhood home of U.S. Navy fleet admiral Chester W. Nimitz, who was in charge of all naval operations in the Pacific during World War II. For navy veterans, the museum serves as a focal point for their service. Its mission statement highlights its role in "perpetuating the memory of the Pacific Theater of WWII in order that the sacrifices of those who contributed to our victory may never be forgotten."[48] With the purchase of a small plaque, an individual can mark any naval topic of their choosing. A vast range of plaques exhibited honor individuals, air groups, Marine divisions, and vessels.

This Texas institution also houses World War II exhibitions on the island hopping campaigns, the role of submarines, and naval aviation. In addition, all are welcome to visit and shape the outside courtyard full of plaques honoring ships, individual service members, and Marine and army land units. For example, one such plaque, including an image of their former ship, was purchased by the Liscome Bay Association to remember their sinking and loss of their carrier. The top of the plaque states, "Dedicated to the officers and men of the Liscome Bay and Squadron VC 39 who placed their lives in harm's way in the name of freedom."[49] It concludes with, "You are not forgotten."[50] In this museum courtyard the general public, unconnected with the governing body of the institution, are granted freedom to shape exhibition.

Interpreting Death

On Pier 86 of the Hudson River, on the west side of Manhattan, is the Intrepid Sea, Air, and Space Museum complex that in a singular space tells multiple stories. Of all these stories, the most powerful exhibition is in the climate-controlled hangar deck, on the exact location of a place of death. While the coordinates of the official battle report on the death of sixty-nine sailors on November 25, 1944, will state an area of operations in the Pacific, the surviving sailors of the attack will think of the *Intrepid*'s hangar deck and those shipmates that fought and died. "Kamikaze: Day of Darkness, Day of Light" is a demonstration for the museum field of a multimedia experience merging seamlessly with quality storytelling on the site of death.

Visitors stand on the spot where the majority of the officers and men died fighting the horrific fires caused by two kamikaze suicide attacks. One of the Japanese planes, in penetrating the hangar deck with fire and heat, placed the entire vessel and its crew at risk in starting a conflagration with the fuel and weapons on board. Sailors realizing the danger to the *Intrepid* and their shipmates dove into smoke and flames to save both.

While the multimedia is over ten years old at the time of this writing, the collection of media forms is impressive and includes lighting controls, five retracting screens with projectors, audio, and smoke and flame effects. The press release reads, "All systems combine to create an immersive, on-location environment experience that tells the history of the kamikaze attacks in a gripping and memorable way."[51] The ten-minute experience is amazingly well designed in that it is unimposing and does not interpret the flow of people in the hangar deck. The only portion of the exhibit on the floor is a semicircle about twelve feet in width, which appears black but in fact electrically lights up the names of those killed on board at the conclusion of the presentation. With retracting screens and other multimedia hanging from the ceiling, many visitors simply walk right past, unaware of its existence, if a scheduled showing is not on. However, when the show is announced over the PA system, a gathering of guests stand next to a World War II–era Avenger single engine torpedo/bomber. This type of aircraft, among dozens of others loaded with combustible fuel and weapons, stood close by at the time of crisis.

Your guide on this experience is an actor who was filmed in color and shown on one of the screens and tells of being a New York City firefighter before the war. He talks about the importance of firefighting on carriers and leading men into the flames to save shipmates and ship. Alarms scream and other audio recreates the yelling of firefighters battling the blaze with hoses. Smoke machines and lighting add to the experience. Our narrator describes the battle, and how the Japanese witnessing the smoke billowing into the blue Pacific sky from miles away chalked up the *Intrepid* as lost. However, she was not, and after being saved and refitting in the United States and returning to the war, the Japanese Navy called her the Ghost Ship, as she seemed to be resurrected from the dead.

Our narrator, in closing, however, gives the cost of saving the carrier, this being his life and that of sixty-eight other sailors. Then names are read aloud from a range of different speakers, voices, and levels of volume. As this occurs, on the unsuspecting black memorial wall individual names light up to list those sailors killed on November 25, 1944. This powerful experience personalizes an event, bringing both the human cost and the fact that his ship was a weapon and not a museum to life. An additional factor is the inclusiveness of the memorial wall in containing more than just sixty-nine names because it lists all the sailors who died serving on board *Intrepid* from the Second World War into the 1970s.

Best Practices and Suggestions for Better Interpretation

- Exemplifies the linkage of the global topic of World War II with the local history of New York City with an actor playing an individual sailor who perished in the kamikaze attack narrating the presentation.
- Demonstrates an exhibition that does not overpower a given space; it simply blends into the surrounding interpretation when the presentation is not on display.
- Inclusive memorialization in not only remembering those sailors lost during World War II but in the entire service history of the *Intrepid*.

SS *American Victory*

In the article "A Golden Age for Historic Properties," the authors John and Anita Durel argue that while recent times have been very difficult for cultural institutions of all shapes and sizes, the best times are ahead for historic properties willing to change. A key aspect of their argument is the wave of upcoming baby boomer retirees transforming the definition of retirement. Rather than just golfing and walking in circles around malls, the Durels argue these individuals will seek out cultural institutions to donate their valuable time and skills. The Durels suggest for institutions willing to change and share authority that the best days are yet to come. This ecumenical approach, of thinking of historic properties as places were many people can have authority as opposed to just the curator, the article sums up with a single bullet point: "Stop thinking of 'interpretation' and start thinking of 'facilitation.'"[52]

This excellent article makes another important point: "Stop focusing only on the intellectual and social content of the experience, and start including spiritual content."[53] It is this point that has the most potential for naval exhibitions. Rather than just listing naval engagements or the specifications of a particular classification of war vessel, seeking to resuscitate the human emotions of fear, anger, and excitement holds extraordinary opportunities in naval interpretation. A prime example of a naval museum seeking to explore spiritual content is seen at the SS *American Victory*.

Located on the waterfront in Tampa, the SS American Victory is one of only four fully operational World War II–era vessels in the United States. Launched from a California shipyard in 1945, she cost $2.5 million to construct. In her first voyage, she circumnavigated the globe, first hauling supplies to ports of call in Southeast Asia, then the Indian Ocean, and finally crossing the Atlantic and returning to America. Later she functioned as a cargo vessel in both the Korean and Vietnam conflicts. Decommissioned and threatened with being cut up for scrap, a movement for her preservation landed her in Tampa, where she received a $2 million restoration. The stated mission of the American Victory Ship Mariners Museum is "to honor the dedicated men and women who provided service during times of peace and war."[54]

Touring this vessel contrasts sharply with other ship-based museums as very little of the *American Victory* is off limits. Walking on board, the division between exhibition space and public space is seamless as visitors explore the ship at their own pace and on a path of their own making. Nearly all the nine levels of this 455-foot-long vessel are wide open in terms of safe access. Groups of families explore the three-level cargo holds, gyro rooms, and use original bathrooms. While walking the galley visitors notice that a coffee pot is on and coffee cups of different colors and sizes hang from the ceiling nearby, hinting at the employees and volunteers associated with the ship.

She is a symbol for something much better than just this individual victory ship named after American University in Washington, D.C. As the mission statement says, "We are a world-class, shipboard, maritime museum dedicated to honoring the men and women who built, sailed, protected and provided service, worldwide, through the American Merchant Fleet since 1775 during times of peace and war."[55] It is in this vein that this site represents something bigger than just one ship, just like individual sailors are a part of something greater then themselves, which is a key to organizational success today. As a civic platform, this vessel follows the Durels' notion of facilitation rather than interpretation.

Partnering organizations using the *American Victory* as an educational platform include the local school district and the University of South Florida. Beyond educational in the formal sense, the vessel serves in training local first responders and also canines used by the FBI and the U.S. Custom and Border Protection.[56] Walking the different levels as a visitor and seeing the original functioning ships bridge with navigational maps of Tampa Bay laid out points to the fact that this is a unique exhibition. This is a ship in a true sense, completely functioning in its originally designed role.

Figure 4.5. SS *American Victory* open daily in Tampa, Florida, is one of just a handful of fully functioning World War II–era vessels that still takes visitors out to sea. Photo by Ben Hruska.

Walking around the vessel, a door is seen down a dark corridor. Pushing the hatch door open, a flood of light exits, along with the hum of mechanical movement. Entering into this space, you step onto a see-through walkway made of steel. Beyond the noise, the smell of fuel oil gives away the fact that this is not a stationary display like on most historic vessels. Staring down between their feet, past the coiling of horizontal and vertical piping, visitors see two engines some twenty-five feet below. This perspective grants a unique view of the ship and also exemplifies how this cultural institution has a "spiritual content." This ship is alive. The six thousand horsepower still allows the 455-foot vessel to cruise at seventeen knots. During the war, it could haul over ten thousand tons of war material; today *American Victory* hauls a different cargo twice a year.[57]

The reader maybe asking why this description of the *American Victory* is under the section of exhibitions, as this cultural attraction lacks clear delineations between spaces for visitors and exhibits. Here you walk in the galley that during the war was used to feed the crew of sixty-two civilian merchant sailors and twenty-eight naval personnel. In doing so, you smell hot coffee and see creamer out for the volunteers and staff manning the ship. The reason for this being considered an exhibition is the two days a year when the *American Victory* steams out of Tampa Bay toward the open ocean. On these days, six hundred visitors are on board, a big band plays live songs from the era such as the Andrews Sisters' "Boogie Woogie Bugle Boy" and Les Brown and his famed version of "Sentimental Journey." Merchant Marine and U.S. Navy veterans from numerous conflicts board with their family members to take a ride on a real World War II vessel. Staff and volunteers, dressed in period uniforms, take in the lines as a tugboat nudges the *American Victory* off the pier. Under her own power, signaling other vessels in the busy port as she enters the main channel into the Gulf of Mexico, she is a one-of-a-kind form of naval exhibition.[58] The Durels' argument for "A Golden Age for Historic Properties" is seen with hundreds gathered around a stage in the large cargo space, singing the hymn of the Merchant Marines. Such events on a moving historic property exemplify their argument, as they write, "Stop focusing only on the intellectual and social content of the experience, and start including spiritual content."[59]

Best Practices and Suggestions for Better Interpretation

- Serves in highlighting the multiple roles a single institution can fulfill, such as exhibition, public commemoration, and motivation of volunteers.
- Demonstrates that ship-based museums need not be forever stationary—these can incorporate the ability to sail the seas into the institution's stated mission.
- Exemplifies public outreach in making connections to veterans groups, local universities, and local governmental agencies.

First Peoples

The last forty years have witnessed a revolution in the methods and means of storytelling in museums and historic sites. The numbers of voices included in the exhibition and historic interpretation has increased, creating a richer mosaic of narratives. Besides the incorporation of aspects of gender and social classes in interpreting history, another worldwide phenomenon has taken place. This is the inclusion of an indigenous voice, and building on this, such groups from all over the world have started to coalesce and work together in facing challenges and celebrating victories. For example, a group founded in 1997 called First Peoples Worldwide seeks to portion out funding to indigenous communities in communicating with governments, NGOs, and international corporations. A core of their mission is: "We facilitate the use of traditional Indigenous knowledge in solving today's challenges, including climate change, food security, medicine, governance and sustainable development."[60]

Rather than just looking at first peoples as perpetual victims, a more nuanced view can be sensitive to past and current wrongs but also see these groups as active participates in shaping and controlling their environment. This includes numerous aspects of naval technological sophistication. As opposed to seeing seas, rivers, and lakes as hindrances to human movement and exploration, indigenous history demonstrates to us the inherent human quality of utilizing innovation in transforming an obstacle into a benefit. From the Iroquois utilization of the

Finger Lakes region in what became upstate New York to the Maori discovery and settling of New Zealand, indigenous peoples have used watercraft in expanding their populations and fishing areas. It is time for us to interpret and display this rich indigenous naval history seen throughout the world.

Teremoe

A groundbreaking example of museology is Te Papa in Wellington, New Zealand. The fact that this is a bilingual nation is seen at this national museum with text on exhibitions and audio components using both English and Maori. The museum is a radical departure from the notion of viewing its indigenous population as the "other" and in need of examination and classification for people who only lived in the past. In viewing the Maori as both active in the past and in today's New Zealand society, Te Papa breaks away from the notion that this indigenous relevance only belongs in the history books. A singular object on exhibition at Te Papa, showing the past accomplishments while simultaneously demonstrating the significance of the Maori today, is seen in a watercraft.

The craft is over sixteen meters long and has the capacity to hold up to forty warriors. The front portion of the canoe ornately describes the Maori creation story. Like a central component in many creation stories, a binary is seen in this vessel, with portions of carved hardwood depicting the worlds of light and dark and father sky and mother earth. On the very front of the bow, mirroring Viking dragon ships of the Baltic, Tumatauenga, the god of war, is guiding the way forward into battle. The importance of the symbolic power of animals for the Maori is seen in the carving, such as the albatross and the kahu (New Zealand hawk) whose feathers are depicted on the teremoe. The vessel is constructed from a single trunk of a species of tree known locally as the totara tree.

Viewing the ornate craftsmanship of such a vessel, it is easy to forget that this is a mobile platform for waging war. As the Maori expanded over New Zealand, over the centuries rival tribes would at times come into conflict with each other. However, this exhibition, while highlighting a war canoe, does note that Maori boat building extended well beyond warfare. The majority of Maori canoes were much less detailed in decorative design and smaller and with other purposes such as fishing. Thus, similar to today's connection with aircraft, while some were used in warfare and contain amazingly sophisticated technology, most do not drop laser-guided bombs or break the sound barrier. This exhibition does a sound job in noting that while warfare took place at times in Maori society, the vast majority of the Maori time on the water was spent on other purposes.

This particular vessel was used in battles with British settlers in the mid-1860s, establishing settlements on the Whanganui River. Beyond taking part in the fighting, this vessel was used in transporting dead warriors back to the Maori village. Teremoe was donated to a museum in Wellington in the year 1930, after which a few minor carved aspects, such as new sideboards, were added to make the vessel more decorative. However, other than these small changes, this vessel is a true example of the peak of Maori boat-building technology that had evolved since landing on New Zealand in the eleventh century CE. The vessel is on display with the bottom of the hull at about waist high level for the average visitor, thus allowing close observation of the intricate craftsmanship. As a portion of the permanent exhibition on the fourth floor of Te Papa, the exhibition is incorporated into visitor tours and school group curriculum.[61] This represents a top-notch example of the exhibition of indigenous naval technology and celebrates the accomplishments of the Maori, which includes traversing the vast south central Pacific and locating the last undiscovered place to be inhabited by man.

Native People: Navigating Seas of Change

Located on Vashon Island, Washington, the Vashon-Maury Island Heritage Museum is an all-volunteer organization. While small in scale, the leadership of the organization dreams big and in the production of a 2014 exhibition placed itself within the cohort of the most successful small museums in North America. The exhibition "Native People: Navigating Seas of Change" won awards from the Washington Museum Association and the American Association for State and Local History (AASLH). The main thrust of the exhibit centered on addressing the misconception that the Sxwobabc people, who lived on the island for centuries, just traveling to the sea island in Puget Sound for summer farming as opposed to being year-round inhabitants. The distinction may seem trivial, however, it proved critical in later land claims and also in the greater marginalization of the Puyallup Indians, of which the Sxwobabc were a subgrouping.[62]

Utilizing a mixture of archaeological evidence and oral history, the exhibition demonstrates that the Sxwobabc people resided in communal year-round longhouses composed of cedar. The oral histories were from Lucy Slagham Gerand, who lived from 1836 to 1929, and were conducted by an archaeologist in 1918 and in 1927 during legal courtroom testimony with regard to native land claims. Such compelling evidence teamed up with volunteer help from educators, tribal members, and linguists sheds light onto this neglected aspect of the history of Vashon Island. In addition to exhibition, eight public programs were produced building off the themes found in the exhibit, including tribal storytelling, treaty fishing rights, and the influence of the sea on Sxwobabc artwork. These programs and the exhibit all challenge the notion that these original tribal members only visited this thirty-five-square-mile island for a few months out of the year. Of the exhibit, local author Jean Findlay writes, it was "a symphony of displays that appeal to all the senses. From artifacts such as Lucy's mother's basket, to pictures of events taken at the historic time, to a seasonal calendar geared to how natives identified each season, to an interactive tablet that pronounces Sxwobabc sounds and words, the exhibit is a masterpiece of variety and truth."[63]

Besides the exhibit earning both state and national recognition, tangible benefits followed this success. First, the number of visitors increased, which begot expanded community outreach. Second, after the full exhibition was taken down in 2015, portions of it were broken up for further display. While a core portion remained and was transferred into the permanent display, the other sections were consolidated into smaller traveling exhibitions for use by not only other museums in the state, but also the Puyallup people.[64] The challenging exhibition calling into question the local memory of Puget Sound also challenges those in the field of naval history. More specifically, that North American naval history did not commence with the arrival of Christopher Columbus. Coastlines, estuaries, and bays for indigenous peoples functioned as highways of peoples, ideas, and migrations long before the Columbian Exchange.

Best Practices and Suggestions for Better Interpretation

- These examples demonstrate that indigenous history is not outside the greater bounds of naval history.
- Interpreting indigenous history opens the door to an international approach in interpretation.
- Indigenous history can be used by museums based on all levels of scope, including a national museum and small all-volunteer historical society.

Holistic Approach

Before we close this section on exhibitions, a word of warning about the issue of siloing. An article in *Forbes* magazine defined the silo mentality as "a mindset present when certain departments or sectors do not wish to share information with others in the same company."[65] The majority of scholarship on breaking out of siloed thinking is not centered on museums of course, but instead the fields of administration and business. Siloed management of personnel at large corporations can stifle creativity, and worse, lead to large amounts of wasted time and resources in duplicated work and heated conflict within the organization. As a leading business website states, "Our environment and the opportunities it presents for innovation requires more integrated thinking and cross-functional solutions, but many efforts still occur independently, isolated from others' insights and perspectives."[66] Simply put, factions of employees working against one another as opposed to working together is bad for business.

This section is not suggesting that a silo mentality takes place within the management of our historically minded institutions. However, with a critical eye, a silo effect can still be seen in historical exhibitions. For example, exhibitions can fall into the trap of a laser-like focus on just one topic. With our love of interpreting history to make it relevant for visitors, our products can easily lose the forest for a few individual trees. No matter the topic, whether naval history or any other historical subject, we have all encountered siloed exhibits. No matter how well designed and thought out, with singular focus on one historic topic the visitor loses the outside world. We need to make larger connections to the outside world if we want our exhibitions to be relevant in shaping today's society. Failing to make larger connections, we simply fall into the realm of escapism, that of a historic exhibition with no connection to our daily lives. One way to avoid this trap is to take a holistic approach that weaves history with other humanistic disciplines such as art, music, and the social sciences.

The scholars Virginia Anderson and Lauren Johnson in their work *Systems Thinking Basics* give a definition truly applicable to curators seeking exhibitions that make larger connections to such topics as immigration, climate change, and the human impact on the shaped environment. In defining systems thinking, they write, "a school of thought that focuses on recognizing the interconnections between the parts of a system and synthesizing them into a unified view of the whole."[67] Applied to naval exhibitions, such thinking modeled for large businesses or governments can produce larger big picture exhibitions, allowing visitors to make connections beyond history. Considering these models in knocking down silos within our exhibition layout, we give ourselves the opportunity to harmonize more than just the field of history in reaching exhibition goals. We should not fear history being drowned out by such areas as the natural sciences or architecture looking at the built environment, but view our field of mastery as one apart from the greater field of the humanities. In considering such an act, two exhibitions demonstrate this methodology in taking historic naval topics to the next level in merging with other disciplines.

The Oakland Museum of California

Our first example is the exhibition "Above and Below: Stories from Our Changing Bay" produced by the Oakland Museum of California that germinated from the tearing down of a bridge. With the removal of the eastern half of the Old Bay Bridge, which required five years to complete, both state and federal historic preservation laws required steps to mitigate the cultural loss of the seventy-seven-year-old structure. The Oakland Museum was contacted about the possibility of designing and fabricating an exhibition on the history of the bridge as part of the mitigation process. While the museum thought an exhibit centrally focused on the bridge was too narrow a subject, it did see possible success in an exhibition on the changing landscape of the bay as a result of the longstanding relationship with man. Promise was seen in expanding the original concept and looking at an environmental history of the greater bay, which is one of the most urbanized estuaries in the world.

The central framework of the exhibition is the field of historical ecology. Using a period of six thousand years, encompassing the human creations of the indigenous shell mounds to modern bridges, man has shaped and been shaped by this bay. On the museum website, the senior curator, Louise Pubols, speaks of scope of the project. She says it centers on "land that is not really considered wilderness but is land in a city that still has nature in it. And, how do we think about nature in a city?"[68] Besides deviating beyond the history field, the exhibit sought to break down barriers in the physical layout of the completed project.

This was the first exhibition at the Oakland Museum to utilize all three gallery spaces, each devoted to art, history, and natural science. With extensive use of multimedia, including oral histories with specialists in a host of fields, the overall goal of the exhibit focused on the bay's history as a means to engage visitors in the present. In using periodization, breaking the transforming relationship of the bay and humans into smaller portions to show change over time, it enabled visitors to think about such pressing issues as wetlands restoration, climate change, and invasive species.[69] While not shedding the importance of history, this exhibition can be seen as a model of naval history asking visitors to consider bigger questions about the present. In examining naval history through the stationary frame of a bay, the Oakland Museum produced an award-winning exhibition with an original conception of just viewing a bridge and turning it into an engaging experience looking at the interchange of human engineering and natural forces.

The Detroit Historical Society

Another example of the braiding together of differing topics of inquiry is the exhibition "Built By the River." With the use of the waterways of the Detroit River and nearby lakes, all composed of freshwater, this exhibition challenges the notion that naval and maritime history is an exclusive topic related to the world's oceans. In viewing the importance of the river through three frames of reference, these being social, economic, and ecological, the exhibition explores changes over time for Detroit, all stemming from the strategic location of the Detroit River. The twenty-five-mile-long river, while short on length, is long on commercial and military importance. Linking Lake Erie to the south and Lake St. Clair to the north, and then on to the Great Lake system, the river has been central to the city. The Detroit River is an economic pipeline, a waterway linking Duluth, Minnesota, to the Atlantic Ocean. Simply put, as America evolved by expanding both in physical size and economically, so too did Detroit in keeping up with the maritime requirements of getting these goods out of the Midwest and into the world market.

The exhibition starts with the impact of the fur trade, which suddenly thrust high importance on the geographic location of the section of land west of the Detroit River. Sought after and then later fought over by France and Britain, the European conflict radically altered the lives of native peoples caught between these two forces. With the opening of the Erie Canal in 1825, the commercial traffic on the Detroit River accelerated until it became the busiest waterway in the world. The exhibition, incorporating a broad view, looks across the river and to the relationship with Canada. This includes the heritage of the Underground Railroad with fugitive slaves from the American South using the system of informal abolitionist supporters in escaping the United States. The river used as a method of staying outside the law is also explored with the history of Prohibition and the profitable transfer of Canadian whisky into the United States.

An additional consideration in the fabrication was aligning up portions of the interpretive outline to coincide with the state of Michigan's science and social sciences curriculum. Thus, the dual theme of industry and ecology is seen throughout the exhibit. For example, a recreated canoe serves as a hands-on object for all visitors, young or old.[70] This canoe, placed in the center of the exhibition space, demonstrates a cross-disciplinary object addressing the intersection of humans and their environment, economics, and technology. The canoe can tell many things; as a design it showcases innovation, the materials making up the craft demonstrate humans using their environment, and the object in its entirety places the Detroit River into the greater context of the human relationship in movement using water.

"Built By the River" and "Above and Below: Stories From Our Changing Bay" show the holistic approach to naval history. Exhibitions with a targeted goal of locating the sweet spot of the intersection of three or more subject areas, while challenging, if completed correctly hold huge potential for success. And like the designs for these exhibits, this success will produce benefits on a number of fronts.

Notes

1. Alison Landsberg, *Prosthetic Memory: The Transformation of American Remembrance in the Age of Mass Culture* (New York: Columbia University Press, 2004), 2.

2. Ibid.

3. Suzanne Falgout, Lin Poyer, and Laurence M. Carucci, *Memories of War: Micronesians in the Pacific War* (Honolulu: University of Hawaii Press, 2008), 3.

4. Ibid., 24.

5. Pierre Nora, "Between Memory and History: Les Lieux de Memoire," *Representations* no. 26 (1989): 12.

6. "Battleship Cove Launches Dynamic New Exhibit Reenacting the Attack on Pearl Harbor," PR Newswire, http://www.prnewswire.com/news-releases/battleship-cove-launches-dynamic-new-exhibit-reenacting-the-attack-on-pearl-harbor-127509663.html (accessed May 21, 2015).

7. "La Belle: The Ship That Changed History," Bullock Museum, http://www.thestoryoftexas.com/la-belle/the-exhibit (accessed September 2, 2015).

8. "La Belle Shipwreck," YouTube, https://www.youtube.com/watch?v=zVd0-OOWSt0 (accessed September 2, 2015).

9. "La Belle: The Ship That Changed History," Bullock Museum.

10. "La Belle Shipwreck," YouTube.

11. "La Belle: The Ship That Changed History," Bullock Museum.

12. "Press Information," Bullock Museum, http://www.thestoryoftexas.com/about/press (accessed September 2, 2015).

13. Ibid.

14. "Naval Toys Exhibition," New London Custom House Maritime Museum, visited by author on July 21, 2015, New London, Connecticut.

15. David Clark, "Museum Ship Exhibits: There and Back Again," self-published and given to the author on April, 3, 2014.

16. Ibid.

17. David Clark, "Traditional Museums vs. Ship Museums," self-published and given to the author on April, 3, 2014.

18. Clark, "Museum Ship Exhibits."

19. "Hands-On History Lesson," Patriot's Point Home of the USS *Yorktown*, http://www.patriotspoint.org/explore_museum (accessed August 28, 2015).

20. Clark, "Traditional Museums vs. Ship Museums."

21. Exhibit Panel, "Freshwater Aircraft Carriers," visited by the author on November 11, 2015, Pima Air Museum, Tucson, Arizona.

22. Exhibit Panel, "Nose Art and Insignia: Beyond the Girls," visited by the author on November 11, 2015, Pima Air Museum, Tucson, Arizona.

23. Ibid.

24. Shameem Black, "Commemoration from a Distance: On Metamemorial Fiction," *History and Memory* 23, no. 2 (2011): 60.

25. "ESCAA Museum Information," ESCAA website, http://escortcarriers.com/museums. html (accessed February 1, 2012).

26. Ibid.

27. Ibid.

28. Nicholas J. Saunders, ed., *Matters of Conflict: Material Culture, Memory, and the First World War* (London: Routledge, 2004), 15.

29. Joe Macchia, interviewed by Ben Hruska, October 17, 2011, Tempe, Arizona.

30. "CVE 9 Bogue USN Escort Carrier: Tamiya 1/700," Ship Modeling Mailing List, http:// smmlonline.com/reviews/models/bogue/bogue.html (accessed December 7, 2011).

31. Chris Ballard, "The Ship as Symbol in the Prehistory of Scandinavia and Southeast Asia," *World Archeology* 35, no. 3 (2003): 390.

32. Ibid.

33. James D. Hornfischer, *The Last Stand of the Tin Can Sailors: The Extraordinary World War II Story of the U.S. Navy's Finest Hour* (New York: Random House, 2004), 352–54.

34. "Ship History," USS *St. Lo* Association, http://www.ussstlo.com/contentPage.cfm?ID=455 (accessed January 23, 2012).

35. "The End of a Fighting Ship," USS *St. Lo* Association, http://www.ussstlo.com/content-Page.cfm?ID=414 (accessed January 23, 2012).

36. Ibid.

37. "The Carriers: The List," America's Navy, http://www.navy.mil/navydata/ships/carriers/ cv-list.asp (accessed January 9, 2016).

38. Exhibit Panel, "'Billy' the Moose and Theodore Roosevelt: Onboard USS *Theodore Roosevelt*, CVN 71," visited by author on May 30, 2009, Norfolk, Virginia.

39. "Fact File: Aircraft Carriers," American's Navy, http://www.navy.mil/navydata/fact_display. asp?cid=4200&tid=200&ct=4 (accessed January 11, 2016).

40. Dale L. Walker, *The Boys of 98: Theodore Roosevelt and the Rough Riders* (New York: Forge Book, 1998), 13, 15.

41. Ibid., 21.

42. "Crypt of John Paul Jones," Chaplain's Center: United States Naval Academy, http://www. usna.edu/Chapel/virtualTour/crypt.php (accessed January 9, 2016).

43. "The Two Burials of John Paul Jones," Seacoast New Hampshire, http://www.seacoastnh. com/jpj/burial.html (accessed January 9, 2016).

44. "Re-Internment of John Paul Jones," TheodoreRoosevelt.com, http://www.the-odore-roosevelt.com/images/research/speeches/trjpjburial.pdf (accessed January 9, 2016).

45. "The Two Burials of John Paul Jones."

46. "Re-Internment of John Paul Jones."

47. Ibid.

48. "Home," National Museum of the Pacific War, http://www.pacificwarmuseum.org/Index. asp (accessed February 7, 2012).

49. "Search Memorial Plaques," National Museum of the Pacific War, http://www.pacificwar-museum.org/SearchPlaques.asp?LastLetter=l (accessed February 7, 2012).

50. Ibid.

51. "'Kamikaze: Day of Darkness' Exhibit Returns," Press Releases, Intrepid.org, http://www. intrepidmuseum.org/About-Us/Press-Room/Press-Releases/"KAMIKAZE--DAY-OF-DARK-NESS,-DAY-OF-LIGHT"-EXHIBIT-.aspx (accessed August 17, 2015).

52. John and Anita Durel, "A Golden Age for Historic Properties," *History News*, Summer 2007, 7.

53. Ibid.

54. Pamphlet, "American Victory Ship Mariners Museum: An American Icon and National Treasure," Tampa, Florida, (accessed December 20, 2015).

55. "Welcome Aboard," American Victory Mariners Museum, http://www.americanvictory.org (accessed December 23, 2015).

56. Pamphlet, "American Victory Ship Mariners Museum."

57. "Determining the Facts," Liberty Ships and Victory Ships, National Park Service, http://www.nps.gov/nr/twhp/wwwlps/lessons/116liberty_victory_ships/116facts2.htm (accessed December 27, 2015).

58. Aimee Alexander, "Forever a Merchant Marine," *Tampa Bay Times*, December 22, 2013, 4.

59. Durel, "A Golden Age," 7.

60. "About Us," First Peoples Worldwide, http://www.firstpeoples.org/about-us/about-us (accessed January 20, 2016).

61. "Teremoe," Te Papa: Our Place, http://www.tepapa.govt.nz/Education/OnlineResources/SGR/Pages/Teremoe.aspx (accessed January 21, 2016).

62. "Vashon Island's Native People," AASLH Awards, http://awards.aaslh.org/award/vashon-islands-native-people-navigating-seas-of-change (accessed January 15, 2015).

63. "Sxwobabc Exhibit Wins Awards," The Vashon Loop, http://www.vashonloop.com/article/sxwobabc-exhibit-wins-awards (accessed January 15, 2016).

64. "Vashon Island's Native People."

65. "The Silo Mentality," Forbes, http://www.forbes.com/sites/brentgleeson/2013/10/02/the-silo-mentality-how-to-break-down-the-barriers (accessed January 6, 2016).

66. "Associations Now," Center of Association Leadership, https://www.asaecenter.org/Resources/ANowDetail.cfm?ItemNumber=46320 (accessed January 5, 2016).

67. Ibid.

68. "Above and Below: Stories From Our Changing Bay," Oakland Museum of California, http://museumca.org/exhibit/above-and-below-stories-our-changing-bay?qt-above_and_below=0#qt-above_and_below (accessed January 6, 2016).

69. Ibid.

70. "Built By the River," Detroit Historical Society, http://detroithistorical.org/dossin-great-lakes-museum/exhibitions/signature-exhibitions/built-river (accessed January 11, 2016).

CHAPTER 5

Public Memorials

AN ANALYSIS OF COLLECTIVE MEMORY of naval topics formed in the absence of a particular land-based site must note that public commemoration became more common in the Western world starting in the eighteenth century. Many of these commemorations formed around the construction of a national narrative with the rise of democratic nation-states. Michael Kammen, in his seminal work on American myth and tradition *Mystic Chords of Memory*, explores early examples of these efforts in American commemoration. He writes, "Erecting public monuments to celebrate events, ideas, or heroes began on a broad scale late in the eighteenth century when nationalism and political ideology started."[1] He argues that many of these subjects of monuments formed around national ideals, or an entire conflict, which was not easily placed at a particular site. Thus, an adopted site was reached, allowing visitation by large numbers of people marking such sites of national importance.

According to Kammen, "Public monuments honoring sundry military heroes for their successes in war had essentially been unknown before the French Revolution."[2] Veterans groups played critical roles in the creation of many nation-building monuments focused on military subjects. Kammen notes that in the nineteenth century, groups formed around a diversity of collective memories that encompassed individual units, regiments, and whole armies. In 1868, Civil War veterans of the Union Army formed the Grand Army of the Republic (GAR) and successful lobbied for the observance of Memorial Day.

Kammen exhibits the breadth and depth of veterans' actions to express collective memory during the nineteenth century using the vignette of the nation's birthday: July 4,

1888, in New York City. A range of events occurred. The city hosted Civil War veterans conducting exercises in Battery Park. Veterans from the War of 1812 gathered for their annual meeting and lunch. Civil War veterans formed around collective memory paraded in the streets, including individual posts of the GAR and Sons of Veterans, and these groups and thousands of other citizens descended on Grant's Tomb. He writes, "All in all, the day had become a mélange of memories, which perhaps helped to render the chords more mystic."[3] They illustrate how veterans came together to serve as their own public historians long before the term existed. Thus, this self-memorialization by veterans in the American experience is a starting point for modern public historians in understanding public commemoration either in the form of annual ceremony, public dedication, or designated space for remembering. More specifically with regard to this study, those seeking to rescue naval topics from oblivion fostered the construction of public memorials. Faced with their own immortally and seeing the danger of certain naval events receding from living memory like flotsam and jetsam on a city pier, active agents formulated methods of tethering facets of a given society's naval past to civil space, thus grounding certain aspects from the storm of historical amnesia that consumes almost all historic topics given enough time.

Rainbow Warrior

On a winter's evening in July 1985, in Auckland, New Zealand, twin explosions rocked the peaceful waterfront. The targeted attack on a vessel docked in the town's harbor killed one passenger, Fernando Pereira, a father of two and a freelance photographer. The vessel, *Rainbow Warrior*, was the flagship of Greenpeace, an international organization founded in Canada in 1971 with a stated purpose of bringing global environmental awareness to issues including bottom trawling fishing and global warming.[4] The name of the stricken vessel stemmed from a quote of Chief Seattle of the Suquamish people, who said, "When the Earth is sick, the animals will begin to disappear, when that happens, The Warriors of the Rainbow will come to save them."[5]

Evidence later linked the bombing to the French Secret Service (DGSE) in an attempt to stop Greenpeace's planned protest of French nuclear atmospheric testing in the Pacific's Mururoa Atoll. The New Zealand government took this attack very seriously. As reported on a government official site, "While the attack was on an international organization rather than New Zealand itself, most New Zealanders did not make such a distinction."[6]

Inflicted with heavy damage, the *Rainbow Warrior* lay partially submerged in Auckland Harbor. While the attack successfully ended the protesting career of this vessel, it proved a public relations nightmare for the French government. The bombing also produced blowback in galvanizing world opinion against French testing. Thus, in a sense, *Rainbow Warrior* gave her life bringing greater awareness to the issue of nuclear testing. Greenpeace rechristened a second vessel for the one lost, and this memorial sailed for twenty-one years in the fleet of Greenpeace and retired in 2011 after addressing issues such as whaling and radiated oceans. Other memorial methods of the more inventive form will open this chapter on public memorials.

Matauri Bay

Some three hundred kilometers north of Auckland, far from the largest urban center in the nation, is the isolated maritime community of Matauri Bay. This is of ancestral importance to the Maori, the first inhabitants of New Zealand who landed in the eleventh century CE. After traversing the Pacific in ocean-going canoes, the Maori first waded ashore here. Their ancestors, who stressed an ethos of man's careful relationship with the environment, are buried in the cliffs where ocean meets land on Matauri Bay. It is also believed that interred within the cliffs is the first canoe that brought the Maori to this new land. For these reasons, two memorials to the *Rainbow Warrior* would be placed here, for this is the burial ground of ancestral warriors who understood the delicate relationship of mother earth and man.

Chris Booth, a sculptor from New Zealand, designed and constructed a memorial on an open piece of ground atop a volcanic bluff overlooking the islands of Matauri Bay. Booth is an artist who uses holism and seeks to complete projects with as little environmental impact as possible.[7] Thus, knowing the symbolic importance of the volcanic bluffs, which the Maori view as the resting place of their ancestors, Booth selected a single ten-thousand-pound hexagon pillar that had fallen onto the beach below to serve as the center of the monument he constructed on the cliff top above.

Over two years Booth labored on this memorial, which in a public space would mark the loss of *Rainbow Warrior*. Central to the design is an arch ten meters wide formed with sixty-six large rounded basalt boulders, with a peak some seven meters high, which connects at the top of the single vertically placed large basalt pillar painstakingly moved from the beach below. Centered on the pillar is the large worn propeller of the *Rainbow Warrior*. In an interview at the dedication, Booth addressed the meaning and purpose of this public space that rests upon a site of specific importance to the indigenous Maori. He said, "I want children to come up here and ask their parents questions . . . they look up and say, 'Wow, what was that propeller up there for?'"[8] This in turn would allow parents to speak of the ship, Greenpeace, and the mission of the crew in seeking a nuclear-free Pacific.

Overlooking the stunning panoramic view of bay, the visitor sees two ground-set plaques, one for each language of this bilingual nation, Maori and England. These both read,

> A tribute to the *Rainbow Warrior*
> and her crew in their endeavours
> for peace, conservation and
> a nuclear free planet.
> Dedicated by the Governor General
> His Excellency the Most Reverend
> Sir Paul Reeves, 15 July 1990[9]

Figure 5.1. Chris Booth's commemorative sculpture to Greenpeace's *Rainbow Warrior* surrounded by onlookers during the dedication and Maori blessing at Matauri Bay, New Zealand. Photo by Gil Hanly. Courtesy of Chris Booth.

Ocean Reef as Memorial

A second invented memorial rests within the very waters of Matauri Bay itself. It lies thirty meters under the ocean's surface and is a mosaic of sponges, colorful corals, and an assemblage of goatfish and moray eels. The canvas is the *Rainbow Warrior*, with two large jagged wounds still visible on the starboard side, and the credited artist of this memorial is mother ocean. The wreck, placed here in 1987 two years after the attack, lies in the white sands under Matauri Bay between the small islands of Horonui and Matutapere. Placed in a dive-friendly location, she can be reached by experts and novice divers alike, as her superstructure is just fifteen meters from the surface. Sea life has reclaimed her, as marine plants clinging to her include anemones and differing shades of algae.

Transformed into a complex marine ecosystem, she is also a public memorial and a year-round diveable site that honors the stated mission of the *Rainbow Warrior*. While the bombs did end her working career as a ship patrolling the oceans seeking to bring awareness to environmental issues, she still cruises on a mission marking the beauty of life on planet earth. She also demonstrates the amazing human invention of transforming tragedy into a force of good by placing a wreck, a destroyed ship, in a location of ancestral importance to New Zealand and letting mother nature transform her into a work of art. The United Kingdom's *Daily Telegraph* listed *Rainbow Warrior* as one of the top-ten dives in the world.[10] And divers say, with a bit of imagination, resting on the sandy bottom of Matauri Bay thirty meters underwater, she looks like she is sailing once again. And in a sense she is.

Digital Memorial

Finally, *Rainbow Warrior* is commemorated in a form of place and space that challenges conventional norms of our field. This place is everywhere and nowhere simultaneously, as this is a virtual memorial visited online. Beyond a website just simply displaying photos of the wreck, and text explaining the ecosystem now enveloping it, a Greenpeace online exhibition invites the viewer to experience the memorial to *Rainbow Warrior* by taking a digital dive in Matauri Bay. Visiting the memorial website, the voice of Bunny McDiramid, the executive director of Greenpeace New Zealand, welcomes you in a scuba suit and floating in a dingy above the wreck. She narrates a brief history of *Rainbow Warrior*, including the bombing, her mission at the time, and the memorial in the waters below. She then invites you to join her thirty meters below and explore. A small white propeller spins on your screen, serving as a prompt to enter the water. Clicking on this, Bunny gears up and falls into the water, and we follow her down.

Audio of a breathing regulator is heard, and out of the blue mass, the *Rainbow Warrior* appears. The voice of a male narrator discusses the wreck as we approach the bow of the vessel; he gives us a choice of going left or right, and again white propellers prompt us to begin our journey by exploring either the port or starboard sides. Coral and marine plant life encircle the wreck. Large solitary fish and more social schools engulf portions of the diver's view. Going starboard presents a view of the two holes in the hull from the planted French explosives. Exploration is up to each individual website visitor, allowing investigation of eco-systems now claiming the quarterdeck, wheelhouse, and bridge. To bring context to what the viewer is witnessing, the website includes features on the margins of the screen that allow you at any time to see your position in relation to the wreck from the surface. In addition, a detailed timeline, titled "A Voyage of No Return," brings context to the larger story and the mission of the *Rainbow Warrior* and explains the build up to events, including nuclear testing by the United States and France in the Cold War and the role of Greenpeace. The timeline also completes a secondary task beyond granting context: it reminds the viewer that the amazing scenery of this maritime ecosystem, while stunning, is in fact a memorial, resulting from a targeted attack by a nation-state against a nonviolent environmental organization.[11] This digital memorial, combined with the design of Chris Booth atop the bluffs and the wreck of the *Rainbow Warrior*, demonstrates originality in the conceptual designs of memorialization of maritime topics.

San Diego

Collective efforts with an ecumenical approach memorialize more than just one ship or specific battle. In San Diego, for example, stands a public space commemorating not a specific aircraft carrier, but all carriers spanning the technological gulf from the pioneering USS *Langley*, CV 1, to the modern nuclear-powered USS *Theodore Roosevelt*, CVN 71. This concept of framing memorials around the history of all aircraft carriers, not just one, developed in the early 1990s and led to the formation the Aircraft Carrier Memorial Association.[12] The movement to establish a public space, centered by a stone monument, germinated with the passing of large numbers of the early carriers' crewmembers, including World War II–era sailors. No matter which specific carrier they served on, the veterans recognized that only five of the World War II–era carriers remained of the ninety-nine that existed at the close of the war. With less than 5 percent of the carriers surviving as a testament to their experience, this association gathered momentum in leaving behind a stone monument to all carriers and former crewmembers, who were dying at an accelerating rate.

Located near the waterfront in San Diego, the site is official known as the Naval Aircraft Carrier Memorial. Situated between the Navy Pier and G Street, this space holds symbolic meaning for crewmembers of these vessels as it overlooks a homeport of carrier aviation and the modern-day Pacific fleet. Also, near the Navy Pier, many of the 164 carriers etched into the stone memorial, while in service, docked nearby and off loaded crewmembers heading home. Combined, these two aspects added meaning to this particular space. As a promotional brochure for the site noted, "From its vantage point, visitors can gaze across San Diego Bay and see today's mighty flattops at North Island, preparing for future missions in support of peace and freedom all over the world."[13] While the vast majority of decommissioned carriers listed on the stone memorial were scrapped, this public space linked these veterans' past experiences to the greater history of the U.S. Navy and the modern-day carrier operations.

The memorial itself consists of three parts. First, the black stone obelisk standing nine feet in height lists all the aircraft carriers ever commissioned.[14] A human component is added to the memorial with two bronze sculptures, one of a sailor standing with his sea bag and the other a naval aviator who is on one knee, holding his helmet. Three sides of the obelisk list the individual carriers and text marking the meaning of the carriers fills the fourth. In part, it states, "Powered by the human soul, these ships changed the course of history."[15]

The dedication of the final part of the memorial, the bronze naval aviator, took place in September 1996. In attendance was John Finn, who won the Congressional Medal of Honor for his actions during the attack on Pearl Harbor and later served on the USS *Hancock*, CV 19. Besides attending the dedication, Finn donated money for the $135,000 memorial. A reporter asked Finn about the meaning of the monument. He stated, "It's easy for guys to sit around in a bar and tell lies."[16] The talk Finn spoke of, that of veterans speaking of their wartime experiences in expanded feats of daring, was in danger due to deaths of veterans. As he noted, "All the officers and men I knew and served with are gone like a covey of quail."[17] What died with this generation of veterans was the oral method of remembering their carriers. However, the memorial in a public space transcended the deaths of both the ships it honored and the rapidly decreasing number of crewmen who served on them. As Finn stated, "A person comes along and looks at this and maybe you don't even give a dang. But maybe you read the words."[18]

This constructed memorial symbolizes all the aircraft carriers ever commissioned by the U.S. Navy. The anthropologist Fabio Gygi theorized on this topic in writing about monuments to the Great War. He writes, "To work, they must reduce the complex outside world into some kind of order."[19] The Naval Aircraft Carrier Monument, with an obelisk and a statue of a sailor and pilot, accomplished this goal of reducing the experiences of 164 carriers into a single space. In addition, and perhaps more importantly, Gygi suggests that an additional benefit of a monument is that it outlives those who dedicate it. He writes, "The fact that material things remain, that they outlive their creators and possessors seems to prolong the life of those they actually leave behind."[20] For World War II veterans such as Finn, providing financial support for the construction of the monument and attending the dedication gave him a chance to leave a marker behind. Their ships were gone, but not their memories.

Vessel of History

Veterans of the USS *Gambier Bay*, CVE 73, accomplished a range of memorial feats in the 1970s and 1980s and continued the tradition in the early 1990s when another opportunity presented itself. On July 4, 1992, the U.S. Navy hosted the commissioning of her newest nuclear-powered aircraft carrier. Christened the USS *George Washington*, in honor of the nation's first president, the connection for the veterans of the *Gambier Bay* was the hull number. Whereas their small escort carrier, CVE 73, had a wooden flight deck, this new carrier CVN 73 claimed a steel flight deck of over four acres.

The historian Efraim Sicher, in writing about post-memory and the Holocaust, theorized about the construction of collective memory. In his discussion, he writes, "identity needs to be anchored in a time and place."[21] For the CVE 73 veterans, the commissioning of CVN 73 granted them the opportunity to morph their experiences into the U.S. Navy and the larger traditions of the aircraft carrier. While this particular space, a ninety-thousand-ton carrier, was not stationary, it did represent the permanence in an open space this group of naval veterans sought.

For veterans of the *Gambier Bay*, their wartime experience was unanchored; they lacked a ship and a land-based location to dedicate a memorial. As the first captain of the $1 billion nuclear carrier wrote in welcoming those attending the commissioning, "*George Washington* will serve our country for 50 years as a roving ambassador and symbol of American technological, industrial, and military strength."[22] In attending the commissioning, these *Gambier Bay* veterans in their seventies presented a tangible gift to the young crew of the new carrier, one that symbolized their connection to this new carrier. Housed within the vessel this gift would serve as a link in the greater chain of the U.S. Navy's long tradition of the aircraft carrier.

The veterans of CVE 73 had previously commissioned a painting of their vessel showing the *Gambier Bay* in its final action, with Japanese shells slamming into her unarmed hull and also throwing up geysers of saltwater. This painting commemorated an experience that up until then had only existed in memory. For this newest painting, in an adaptation of meaning, the *Gambier Bay* veterans commissioned the same artiest, R. C. Moore, to depict the newest carrier in the fleet of the U.S. Navy. Moore's painting shows the USS *George Washington*, CVN 73, rolling into large seas with modern F-18 Hornet fighters strapped to her deck.[23] This gift from the crewmembers of one carrier to those of another who shared the same hull number spanned the nearly fifty years between the vessels. Through this they claimed a space and retained a channel to the U.S. Navy and the modern-day carrier force.

Seat as Memorial

Memorialization can take many forms. A range of incidents can spark the creation of naval memorials including battles, admirals, and individual sailors. Serendipity can also have a role at times. Chance encounters decades after conflicts bring not only veterans together, but also their descendants. Recently at the Intrepid Sea, Air, and Space Museum in New York City such an occurrence happened as family members of two deceased sailors, who were good friends during the war, happened to meet as the result of a curator recognizing a wartime photo.

Karoline Nurse's father died in 2007; however, she still elected to attend a seventieth anniversary event of her father's ship, which included veterans and families with a connection to the USS *Intrepid*. Karoline not only attended the 2013 event, but also brought a collection of meticulously documented scrapbooks of her father's. A curatorial staff member examining the images noticed one image taken in London of a group of sailors at Piccadilly Circus. The staff member had seen this exact same picture from a sailor named Anderson, who happened to be labeled on the back of Karoline's father's image. While the Anderson family was not in attendance, Karoline gained their contact information.

Later she confirmed a number of things speaking with the Andersons. Her father and their father, Robert P. Anderson, were very good friends, and Robert was a groomsman in her parents' wedding. She also learned that the Andersons were participating in the Seat of Honor program aboard the *Intrepid*, which allowed for the dedication of a single seat to an individual veteran in the museum's theater on board the ship. The Anderson family also made plans to attend the Memorial Day event on board the ship and witness the unveiling of these new seats of honor: simple elegant nameplates fastened on the top of theater seats bearing a veterans name, serving as a living memorial. That is, these dedicated memorials will be used on a daily basis in educating visitors on the history of the *Intrepid*.

Hearing of the program, Karoline also decided to dedicate a seat, and after contacting the museum staff had it arranged that her father's seat be adjacent to Robert P. Anderson. Karoline attended the dedication of the seats and met all the Andersons. Their fathers' friendship, cemented during the war, proved strong enough for their names to be side by side in the museum made from the hull they served on. As for this memorial's meaning, Karoline wrote, "I can't tell you how meaningful it was to put my father's name on a piece of the ship that meant so much to him."[24]

Ship's Reunion: The Next Generation

Reunions of veterans are powerful things. Once the conflict concludes, most veterans of all wars rarely see the people they experienced one of the foundational events of their lives with. In their youth, brought together by chance, together they survived ordeals both big and small, and some did not survive. When reunions take place decades later, all those thoughts and feelings finally establish an outlet. From my personal experience as a historian, as a young nonveteran two generations removed from World War II, it took me sometime to understand what was occurring attending naval reunions. Like someone first learning chess by watching people play in a park, you think you understand the complexity, then a move happens and all you know is that you are still grappling with a mosaic of meanings. There are many angles and many possible moves, and much more going on than just thinking just one or two moves ahead.

So too with naval reunions, which increase in complexity as multiple generations attend, including children and grandchildren. A glimpse into the complexities of such events was seen at the 2013 reunion in New York City on the Intrepid Sea, Air, and Space Museum, which was open to all sailors who served on the *Intrepid* from 1943 to 1974 and their family members. Those attending could include those who may feel like outsiders at first, as they were searching for a connection to the ship from a family member lost in a war before they were even born.

First, for the former sailors returning to the ship, this proved a powerful experience. Ray Stone, a radioman from 1943 to 1945, felt a range of emotions, including excitement in seeing his ship and sadness in remembering those sailors lost on board as the result of a kamikaze attack. Speaking after visiting the hangar deck, which is now exhibition space, Stone recalled that fateful date. To a reporter he said, "I can still see the bodies. I lost 26 guys. That is a vivid memory I can't forget."[25]

With the deaths of World War II servicemen increasing in the 1990s, for those reunions that still took place more and more attendees included widows and children of deceased veterans. These reunions allowed the (now adult) children to hear firsthand from those still alive about wartime experiences from a loved one's ship. As a curator of the *Intrepid* correctly noted, "Some of the sons and daughters, now adults, said their dads never talked about their time on the ship. The floodgates opened at the reunion, and stories that would have been lost to history were told."[26] As a whole, I think museum professionals are well aware of the power of veterans' reunions in developing a range of successes, including oral histories and soliciting donations of artifacts. However, there is one aspect that I think we as a group can easily overlook: while small in number, family members seeking a connection to a relative who died before their birth is fertile ground for public historians.

How do you remember a loved one you never met? We all have family members we just missed meeting as a result of death. For me, my great-grandfather, a doughboy in World War I, passed away a year before my birth. You hear stories, see images, or maybe even are told you have a similar smile, but you will never meet them on this side of existence. But wars create another paradox: What if that relative is taken away in the flower of youth in war? How do you mourn? How do you say goodbye to someone you never met? Or who was lost at sea in a war that occurred just before your birth? The answer, or one of the answers, was found at the 2013 *Intrepid* reunion, and this occurrence at a public memorial demonstrates the dynamic explorations of family history that can occur at naval reunions.

One of the attendees invited was Sherida Daley, who had many questions about an uncle she had never met. She brought with her one of the few tangible artifacts that proved her uncle's existence, this being an official letter from the U.S. Navy regrettably informing the family of his loss. Sailor Alphonse Moscaritolo was killed by a Japanese torpedo attack, the letter informed, and subsequently was buried at sea. The family would never accept the delivery of any remains. For Ms. Daley, growing up with pictures of the uncle she would never know, this pilgrimage to his ship and visiting with those who also served on her uncle's ship produced strong connections. Conversations at the reunion rendered tales and memories for Sherida about the uncle she never met in life. As she said later, "Until my visit to *Intrepid*, my uncle had been a picture on a wall, a story, a name on a telegram. . . . The homecoming weekend made him real to me."[27] This public memorial facilitates the gathering of reunions. Rather than the nineteenth-century model of public parks and statues just functioning as locations of pigeons and city residents, the *Intrepid* demonstrates an active model of public memorials.

Best Practices and Suggestions for Better Interpretation

- Illustrates the numerous roles ship-based museums can complete such as exhibition and interpretation, but also commemorative space for those seeking a link to a deceased family member.
- Showcases the intimate role all museums can have for visitors.

The U.S. Navy Memorial and Naval Heritage Center

Creating a single public space to commemorate the U.S. Navy, which, founded in October 1775, is older than the national government of the United States and covers America's first foreign engagement in the Barbary Wars into the twenty-first century, is a massive undertaking. Located on Pennsylvania Avenue in Washington, D.C., halfway between the White House and the U.S. Capitol, the U.S. Navy Memorial, like the very mission of the navy, completes a number of aims. The site being in a very compact area and replicating a vessel at sea accomplishes duties simultaneously, such as memorializing, educating, hosting ceremonial events, and serving as an archival focal point. Just as a single vessel can house, feed, wage war, and sail in high seas all at the same time, the design of the U.S. Navy Memorial and Naval Heritage Center successfully memorializes naval history using a number of methodologies.

First, the most visible aspect adjacent to Pennsylvania Avenue is the memorial plaza. Centered on the ground of this public space is the Granite Sea, the largest stone-made map of the world in existence with a diameter of one hundred feet. This area hosts year-round ceremonies, such as the Blessing of the Fleets ceremony in April, the Battle of Midway Commemoration in June, and the navy's birthday in October. Fountains and pools align the circumference of the globe, along with sculptural panels highlighting celebrated acts of naval heroism, both individual and collective. However, one simple statue in particular has come to symbolize the entire site.

A statue standing in solitude is titled *The Lone Sailor*. Designed by Stanley Bleifeld, this piece is featured on postcards and information brochures around Washington, D.C. With hands tucked into his jacket and collar up against the elements, this lone sailor stands watch, and thus honors all U.S. Navy sailors in all American wars. The memorial itself describes it with "he stands in honor of all people who have ever served, are serving now, or are yet to serve in the Navy and Sea Services."[28] While the largest map of the world made of granite and *The Lone Sailor* draw a great deal of attention from tourists walking down Pennsylvania Avenue, this site offers much more than just these two well-photographed markers. Just to the east of both is the entrance to the Naval Heritage Center.

Opening the doors and entering, visitors are welcomed by a receptionist giving information on what is available at the Naval Heritage Center. Down a circular set of stairs into the main portion of the center is the first memorial inside this enclosed space. Set inside sections of curved class are etchings of specific vessels representing a unique form of an annotated timeline with differing classifications of naval history from the age of sail to nuclear propulsion. Further down the staircase, a short history of the service branch is revealed through vessels, from the first original six frigates commissioned with the Naval Act of 1794 down to today's aircraft carriers with four acres of flight deck space.

Once downstairs, naval heritage is memorialized in different methods in one location. The Gallery Deck includes a rotation of exhibitions, the Burke Theater grants seating to over two hundred visitors, the Navy Log Room provides touchscreen kiosks for researching individual sailors, and a media resource center provides access to a small mountain of printed, audio, and video documentation. However, we will examine just one inclusive aspect of this national memorial with memorialization shaped by service members and their families.

Figure 5.2.   Along Pennsylvania Avenue in Washington, D.C., the statue of *The Lone Sailor* watches over the U.S. Navy Memorial. Photo by Ben Hruska.

The Commemorative Plaque Wall defines the word *ecumenical* and allows anyone the opportunity to honor specific ships, air squadrons, or individuals in areas of the military including the U.S. Navy, Marine Corps, Coast Guard, or Merchant Marine. An application system allows purchased plaques to memorialize beyond just text with a grayscale image, thus incorporating a visual aspect of honoring. These plaques are not only publicly displayed at the Naval Heritage Center, but also digitally, allowing for worldwide access to this already very democratic form of memorialization. In addition, plaques, measuring seven by three and three quarter inches, can be personalized with text, logos, and group insignias. Lastly, all sponsors have the opportunity to host a dedication ceremony for the plaque in the Burke Theater, allowing reunion and family groups to personally share their small slice of naval heritage surrounded by the greater history of the U.S. Navy.[29] Thus, a memorialization event for the dedication of the plaque includes a visit to the nation's capital, the U.S. Navy Memorial, and seeing the Memorial Day events on the National Mall. While small in area, these plaques function in giving memorial space for those interested in preserving their naval connection, whether this is an individual sailor, vessel, or air squadron.

Battle of the Atlantic Place

The seminal multivolume work devoted to the overall Allied naval operational perspective of World War II was written by a Harvard-educated U.S. Navy officer. Samuel Eliot Morison's fifteen-volume *History of United States Naval Operations in World War II* took nearly twenty years to complete. With regard to the Battle of the Atlantic, Morison devoted two full volumes to the Allied effort in combating the German U-Boat menace. In the preface to the tenth volume, he describes this campaign as "subject to constant ups and downs, and fought on three levels—on the surface of the ocean, under the sea, and in the air, a war fought by scientists, inventors, naval construction and ordinance experts, as well as by sailors and aviators."[30]

It was said that this was the only theater of the war that interrupted British prime minister Winston Churchill's sleep. In short, if successful, the Battle of the Atlantic guaranteed American-made supplies would reach Britain and the USSR. Failure would sever this lifeline for defeating Nazi Germany. It is ironic then that many history textbooks in secondary schools avoid the Battle of the Atlantic, in part because it has no single large-scale event, such as D-Day, to provide a vehicle for greater meaning to coalesce around. As Morison writes, "An engagement, which goes on so long, is so devoid of spectators and correspondents, and is so far to the rear of the battle lines is apt to recede in memory with the passage of time, for it lacks the classical unities of the drama, being neither one in place nor in time nor the action."[31]

However, currently a bold campaign is underway to invent a specific land-based location to this theater, which currently lacks a singular public space for remembrance, that lasted from 1939 to 1945 and littered the Atlantic's floor with merchant and warships from a host of nations. Called the Battle of the Atlantic Place, this $200 million effort will be on a 4.5-acre piece of waterfront in Halifax, Nova Scotia, and is scheduled to open in 2017 as part of the one hundred-fiftieth anniversary of nationhood of Canada. Proposed architectural plans call for a steel, wood, and glass design, composed of curves and lines, all suggesting a vessel interacting with the ocean. Central to the design is a single large space for a three-sided digital theater. The architectural firm is not billing this as a museum, but as an "experience centre" for a proposed 240,000 visitors annually.[32] They see the experience focusing on stories and visual representations as opposed to objects. The site will include a Memorial Hall dedicated to the thousands of Canadians who perished in this theater of operations. While rejecting the notion of a large collection of objects, the designers are utilizing one single artifact, and she will serve as the centerpiece of the entire experience: Canada's Naval Memorial, the HMCS *Sackville*.[33]

She is a corvette, one of 269 war vessels with the classification. This vessel, amazingly restored to her 1944 configuration, is the only one of these vessels remaining, 123 of which sailed and fought in the Royal Canadian Navy. Corvettes such as the *Sackville* fought in the Battle of the Atlantic from the eastern seaports of Halifax, St. John's, and Londonderry. Composed of riveted iron some two hundred feet long and with a crew of one hundred sailors, the HMCS *Sackville* participated in escorting thirty convoys in the North Atlantic, braving not only German U-Boats, but also brutal sea conditions in winter months. While just one small ship in a very big war, the HMCS *Sackville* has come to symbolize much more for Canadian identity.

Preservation of the *Sackville* stems from a volunteer effort that started in the early 1980s and gained national attention with Canada's cabinet in 1985, declaring her Canada's Naval Memorial. The nation's thousands of families with connections to the Battle of the Atlantic, with this stroke, inherited a singular place to remember. During the war, the costs of this theater were high, with Canada losing twenty-six war vessels, seventy-two merchant ships, and a multitude of maritime aircraft. In short, over five thousand Canadian servicemen died in the theater and their bodies were lost in the Atlantic. She is Canada's oldest warship and thus symbolizes the greater legacy of the Canadian Royal Navy.

She was just a very small part of the overall war effort, but today is under a process of metamorphosis to embody a nation's entire role in the Battle of the Atlantic. As a retired Canadian naval officer wrote, "Sackville's experience was reflected many times over by the hundreds of other Allied warships defending the thousands of convoys trudging eastward against a determined foe or returning westward for more cargo."[34] Her story will then be center stage with the Battle of the Atlantic Place. Encased in a state-of-the-art glass building and surrounded by the three-sided digital theater, she will no longer have two homes exposing her to the elements, one docked in the water for the tourist season and another in dry dock for the brutal winter.

As public historians whose very identity at times is centered on museums, it is easy for architects using such verbiage as "experience centre" to make us uneasy. However, taking a holistic approach and looking at what they are planning, as opposed to the language used, offers hope. While the branding for a $200 million venue in history does not embrace the word *museum*, this is just an issue of semantics. Visitors crave what public historians bring to the table: the singular ability to sift through the gargantuan amount of material culture and paper ephemera on a World War II topic and grant a clear and concise interpretation. This skill set offers hope for our field despite the waves of fashionable terminology that ebb and flow, and that at times reject terms near and dear to our identity. Our talent in bringing meaning to place, especially for ones invented as we see with many naval sites, assures our inclusion in these projects if we seek our rightful place.

Best Practices and Suggestions for Better Interpretation

- A development of a single national museum to function as focal point for remembering a complicated military theater that lasted six years and included multiple nations operating in the Atlantic.
- Demonstrates that the urge to commemorate World War II is not waning in the twenty-first century.
- A single vessel can be integrated into modern methods of storytelling, such as serving as a centerpiece surrounded by a large digital projection screen.

Australian National Maritime Museum

While sites of remembrance can bring meaning to a space, these can complete an additional task of assisting in a municipal redevelopment of an urban center. A principal example of this is Sydney, Australia, which in an attempt to redevelop the waterfront into a cultural destination sought a powerful mechanism for social change, a national museum. The commissioning goals of the Australian National Maritime Museum not only include the telling of the maritime history of an entire nation, but also serve as a driving instrument in a massive redevelopment plan for the urban blight ringing Sydney Harbor.

Opened in 1991, the site history of the museum reaches back to the indigenous Gadigal people using local waters as a major source of protein. The British ushered in European settlement and used the natural shelter that they termed Darling Harhour and Cockle Bay. The settlement of Sydney Cove, acting as the conduit between ocean and land, quickly expanded in size, becoming the largest city in the young continent. Within decades, this maritime settlement transformed into the hub for New South Wales, with railroad tracks, docking facilities, and thousands of immigrants, all of which functioned as logistical magic carpets taking them to settle land somewhere just over the horizon. Rapid change begot rapid change, and after World War II, with tanker ships too big for Darling Harbour, these facilities relocated.[35] Thus, this space of Darling Harbour, with importance for millennia to the Gadigal people and absolutely critical to settlement of New South Wales, rotted into urban and industrial decay.

Today the Australian National Maritime Museum is the premier cultural destination in Sydney's waterfront. With over five hundred thousand visitors annually, it connects visitors with the maritime history of the nation with objects, stories, and public programs. Vessels on display include a replica of Captain James Cook's HMB *Endeavour*, which on its first voyage of discovery (1769–1771) sailed to Australia and New Zealand. This replica recently circumnavigated Australia over the course of thirteen months in an act of public outreach to the rest of the nation. Other vessels on display include a destroyer, the HMAS *Vampire*, former navy patrol boat, the HMAS *Advance*, and a navy submarine, the HMAS *Onslow*. Stressing education, it offers over thirty workshops and tours in a range of curriculum areas for primary and secondary students. One tour and vessel in particular stands out in commemorating and bringing context to the issue of immigration.[36]

A Boat Called Freedom

Docked in Sydney harbor next to a 295-foot submarine from the Australian Navy is *Tu Do*, a small craft fifty feet in length with an engine of just forty-three horsepower. Designed as a Vietnamese fishing vessel and secretly outfitted in 1975 for an exodus leaving the recently invaded South Vietnam by the Communist forces from the north, the small vessel functions today as an educational platform for commemorating the courage of individuals seeking freedom. The museum acquired the vessel in 1990; however, it was not until 1995, after tracking down the original owner, a Mr. Tan Thanh Lu, that the full prominence came into focus.[37] When the story of *Tu Do* (which translates from Vietnamese into *A Boat Called Freedom*) is fully understood, it offers a unique way to discuss the Australian national story of immigration, which is one of the most ethnically diverse nations in the world: one in four residents is born overseas.[38] Combined with a national memorialization on the waterfront discussing national history, this naval-themed educational opportunity challenges and informs schoolchildren and adults alike.

Lu built *Tu Do* as a traditional Vietnamese fishing vessel. He operated it for six months in 1975 to avoid any suspicion from the Communist authorities while he developed a clandestine escape plan. The secret plan called for Lu to fake engine trouble and be towed back to harbor, which allowed him to work on *Tu Do* and not be immediately suspected by surveillance for working on his vessel. This granted him a brief window of opportunity to install a more powerful engine and other modifications for the challenges of open ocean travel. On a dark night, with the *Tu Do* loaded down with thirty-eight people including his pregnant wife, infants, other relatives, neighbors, and friends, Lu embarked on a journey to freedom. Lu avoided detection in escaping Vietnam and the pirates in the Gulf of Thailand that preyed on those fleeing the Communist state. After very brief stops to resupply in Malaysia and Indonesia, this fifty-foot vessel traveled six thousand kilometers and landed two months later near Darwin on the northern coast of Australia.

Mr. Lu's epic journey of immigration to freedom, of crossing an ocean with only a handheld compass and a map torn from a school textbook, brings to life the story behind a small fishing vessel that is dwarfed in scale by the nearby collection of ships. Mr. Lu, on visiting his fishing boat, said, "Making the decision to escape is like going to war. You do it because you think it's necessary, but you never want to do it twice."[39]

In the immigration education program, students examine objects brought to Australia in the 1950s by migrants. Objects handled and discussed in the workshop shed light onto specific migrations to the nation in the 1950s, including a migrant boat called *Orcades*, and also Japanese war brides who married Australian servicemen after World War II. Students gather around a large map placed on the floor, and together trace the journey of those fleeing Southeast Asia. They discuss the pearls associated with ocean travel in crowded boats on the open ocean. With workshop completed, students take two tours, the first of which is to the archives to see objects brought to Australia by children. Second, the school groups walk to the waterfront and tour *Tu Do*. With background knowledge from the workshop and collections tour, students see firsthand a Vietnamese refugee boat that over two months braved the sea with a forty-three-horsepower motor, evaded pirates, and transported over thirty people to freedom.[40]

The Australian National Maritime Museum is a public space created on what was post–World War II urban blight. Conceived as the centerpiece of a strategy in revitalizing a waterfront area, it opened with a bold two-part mission of operating as a site with a devoted mission of telling a national story and also transforming an urban center. Over twenty years after the opening, this institution has fulfilled, and continues to fulfill, this mission. It links historically the nation of Australia with its maritime roots. This museum serves as a prime example of the multiple roles successful institutions can complete in commemoration with any given society.

Charles W. Morgan

In the summer of 2014, the Mystic Seaport Museum in Mystic, Connecticut celebrated the completion of a monumental achievement in naval interpretation. After a five-year restoration effort, the *Charles W. Morgan* sailed south into Long Island Sound on her thirty-eighth voyage. First built in New Bedford, Massachusetts, and launched in 1841, she had an eighty-year career rounding the global in pursuit of whales. While on her first thirty-seven trips she sought whale oil, today she has a new set of goals that her original designers could not have fathomed. First, as the last of the wooden New England whale ships, she symbolizes the nearly three thousand ships in the North American whaling fleet and the whaling industry's two-hundred-year career. Second, the *Morgan*'s thirty-eighth voyage sought what the Mystic Seaport Museum calls "raising awareness of America's maritime heritage and calling attention to issues of ocean sustainability and conservation."[41]

The Mystic Seaport Museum was the ideal organization to complete the restoration of the *Charles W. Morgan*. Founded in Mystic, Connecticut, in 1929 to address the rapidly disappearing seafaring traditions in New England in the first portion of the twentieth century, today it is composed of nineteen acres and has over five hundred historic vessels. With two hundred fifty thousand visitors annually, the organization is a prime example of maritime interpretation in North America. However, interpretation is just one successful facet. The Collections Research Center boosted over forty thousand square feet and houses over two million artifacts. With the use of a recreated seaside village, composed of original historic buildings moved to the site, teamed up with historic interpreters, skilled artisans and educators bring to life New England's maritime traditions. Thus, the *Charles W. Morgan* is a fitting centerpiece of the Mystic Seaport's three-tier educational philosophy of onsite, on board, and online.[42]

In her career as a whaling ship, the *Charles W. Morgan* battled Arctic ice, rounded the Horn of Africa, and braved countless storms. The 106-foot-long vessel boosted three main masts that when fully rigged harnessed over seven thousand square feet of sail. While all impressive aspects in seeking whales, all these facts transformed into liabilities after she retired in 1921, as deterioration and rot set in after retirement. After twenty years of neglect, she came to Mystic Seaport. In 1966, by order of the Secretary of the Interior, she was designated a National Historic Landmark; however, in reality she sat in a berth of sand and mud and was just a shell of her former glory. While located at the premiere maritime heritage institution in the United States, the restoration project of a vessel of this scale was just not organizationally possible; however, the goal of full restoration continued to incubate.

In 2008, the *Morgan* officially started her grand restoration as she was placed in the museum's restoration yards. After a five-year effort rebuilding portions of her keel, bow, and stern, she was deemed ready for her thirty-eighth voyage. She left on May 17, 2014, on a three-month journey around New England to bring attention to maritime heritage and ocean sustainability.[43] One such port was Martha's Vineyard, where many of the *Morgan*'s captains grew up before taking to the sea. When she neared the island, as she slowly exited the June fog, the *Charles W. Morgan* was welcomed with the firing of cannons and blaring of boat horns as a gathered crowd cheered seeing her return for the first time in a century. One such attendee said, "It's a once in a lifetime experience. This must be what it was like for the wives waiting for their husbands to come home."[44] As the only remaining whaling vessel and the oldest commercial ship in the nation, this goodwill tour around New England promoted two different goals of Mystic Seaport. First, it highlighted the over eighty-year mission of the Mystic Seaport Museum, which in a single place protects and memorializes coastal New England history that is all but gone. Second, the thirty-eighth voyage of the *Charles W. Morgan* debuted the reframing of the mission of the vessel from a ship designed to track, kill, and harvest whales to that of an agent promoting maritime conservation. And once back in Mystic after three months, her thirty-eighth voyage was nowhere near complete. She is the flagship of the organization and an anchor of a new exhibition experience titled "Voyaging in the Wake of the Whalers."

For the average visitor, simply to walk the deck of the flagship of the Mystic Seaport and know it is the oldest commercial vessel will hold interest for only a matter of minutes. Additionally, the vessel itself is so far removed from the days it sailed oceans for years at a time seeking whales that most visitors would be adrift at what they are really looking at. What is needed is contextualization, introducing visitors to the how, what, where, when, and most importantly who sailed on the *Charles W. Morgan*. As guest curator Anne Witty said, "The stories in this exhibit braid together people, whales, history, and culture. Here are tales of work and wonder, wealth and poverty, nature and society."[45]

Partnering with the National Endowment for the Humanities, Institute of Museum and Library Services, and National Marine Sanctuary Foundation, the Mystic Seaport Museum has made a conscious choice in pushing past the Victorian-era model of preservation, that being simply saving an object. In "Voyaging in the Wake of the Whalers," visitors witness a purpose-produced series of artifacts, pieces of art, and immersion displays, all of which are combined with context-driven interpretation to produce a quality exhibition for all ages. As the museum describes, "the exhibit pushes past the mechanics of whaling to show the richer and deeper stories of the peoples, places, ships, and whales that impacted and were impacted by whaling since the *Morgan*'s construction in 1841."[46]

The most successful tactic used in bridging the gap between nineteenth-century whaling and today is the interactive portions of the exhibit. A touchscreen information kiosk titled "Dive Deeper," with the use of timelines, videos, and maps, allows visitors in their own methods and pace to explore the history of whaling and whales. Additionally, a database of *Morgan* crewmembers allows visitor the chance to trace a genealogical connection to the vessel. In conveying the global scale of the *Morgan's* story, a three-dimensional projection globe introduces guests to the intersection of marine biology, sailing technology, and the multiethnic backgrounds of those composing the crew of whaling ships.[47] Spending years at sea, dodging massive storms, and the dangers in harvesting whales with a hand-thrown harpoon; all these tales are memorialized with a deeper and crisper meaning for the first thirty-seven voyages of the *Charles W. Morgan*.

Best Practices and Suggestions for Better Interpretation

- Shows the act of reinvention of a retired vessel—a whaling ship designed to hunt whales morphing into a vessel with a mission addressing ocean sustainability.
- Demonstrates a leading museum in field not afraid of taking on a challenging restoration and combining this with unique exhibition and educational programs.
- Linking visitors with the subject matter by allowing access to recorded listings of the *Morgan's* crew to find personal connections.

Reimagining Space

So far we have investigated the invention of public space to memorialize naval history that lacks a land-based location. Complex in nature, such sites can conglomerate layers of meaning over time as differing generations of visitors apply their own significance to memorials. At times, a major shift in meaning can occur and rupture the originally designed purpose and form a completely new memorial. New not in the physical sense, but in the memorial sense, for the public space and memorial does not change in the slightest as the nation-state that produced the memorial can over time get relegated to the trashcan of history. Thus, we need to consider a naval memorial in Germany today that memorizes naval history in the two World Wars and simultaneously is a marker of peace.

The cornerstone of the German Naval Memorial was laid on August 8, 1927, on the site of a dismantled coastal battery in the municipality of Laboe. The site overlooks the locks of the Kiel Canal and commercial traffic that flows through it between the Baltic and North Seas. The driving force behind the memorial was the fiercely patriotic German Naval Association, which like many Germans in the 1920s held strong nationalistic opinions on the causes of losing the First World War. The group's stated purpose was to erect a memorial to all German sailors lost in the Great War. However, an additional motive besides memorializing lost sailors was a call to arms for recreating a strong German Navy, which very much like the site of the coastal battery of the memorial, was dismantled by the occupying Allied forces after World War I.

The design, which took nearly a decade to complete, called for an eighty-five-meter-high tower mirroring a rising flame. The overall design theme was linkage, linking land and ocean, lost sailors and visitors to the memorial, and the weak German Navy of the 1920s with a glorious rebuilt navy of the future. Reenforcing this last point, at the dedication of the cornerstone ceremony, the foundational stone was laid by Admiral Reinhard Scheer, who served as commander in chief of the German High Sea Fleet during the famed 1916 Battle of Jutland. Speaking at the event, Scheer stated, "To German seamens' honour, to Germany's floating arms, may both return."[48]

The theme of reviving military greatness by focusing on past military successes was seen again in 1936 at the dedication of its completion. Dedicated on the twenty-year anniversary of the Battle of Jutland, the opening of the memorial was also an act of the Nazi regime with Chancellor Adolf Hitler in attendance. Additionally, Grand Admiral Erich Raeder, commander in arms of the German Navy, in his speech interpreted the memorial in the vein of Nationalist Socialist ideology as a symbol of recapturing German military might. Hitler did not speak and would never return to the memorial. In fact, he greatly disliked the memorial and called it an "unparalleled item of kitsch."[49] Hitler's dislike, and thus his distance from the memorial, may in fact be a main reason the memorial survived into the postwar period.

The memorial survived World War II unscathed and at the conclusion of the hostilities resided in the British zone of occupation. Memorials with especially strong connections to the Nazis were often destroyed by American, British, French, and Soviet forces after the war. However, for the Marine-Ehrenmal, the British did not view it as a threat; as stated in a British occupation document, the memorial did not "glorify war and the spirit of aggression, but belongs to those whose intention is a personal tribute to the seamen who die for their country."[50] Thus, the reorganized German Naval Association took over the domain of the memorial in 1954.

In the restoration ceremony of jurisdiction of the memorial back to the German people, a shift in meaning took place. In speaking at the rededication, the president of the association, a former U-Boat commander, dedicated it not only to all German sailors killed in both World Wars, but all sailors of all nations killed, including Allied sailors. In conveying his interpretation of an international peace memorial, he stated the following: "In commemoration of all dead German seamen and to our dead enemies."[51] This theme of an ecumenical memorial for all sailors lost at sea was expanded upon fifty years later when the German Naval Association issued a new declaration in a 1996 ceremony. Translated, it stated, "Memorial for all those who died at sea and for peaceful navigation in free waters."[52]

The metamorphosis of seventy years, from the cornerstone laid in 1926 to the rededication in 1996, shows the evolution in the transference in meanings. Designed in part as a marker to Germany rebuilding its depleted navy after the Great War, dedicated by a Nazi official with Hitler in attendance, escaping destruction by the British-occupied force, and finally gifted back to the German Naval Association, the Marine-Ehrenmal has undergone a series of transformations with humans protecting the meaning of a memorial. In its current phase, it is a significant space for understanding international meaning to those lost at sea. This fact is seen visiting the memorial. Walking into the base of the tower and entering the Hall of Commemoration, visitors see wreaths and flowers placed by private groups, individuals, and foreign delegations. Climbing 240 feet up the steps to the top and viewing maritime traffic utilizing the Kiel Canal, one has a fantastic view of not only the sea, but of who this memorial is dedicated to. Flags from a host of nations are dipped when passing the memorial daily, not honoring German sailors or sailors from their own individual nation, but in honoring all sailors, merchant or naval, who died at sea.[53]

Nantes

Located on the western coast of France where the River Loire enters the Bay of Biscay, the city of Nantes was strategically located for success in the period of European history called mercantilism, the era in which European powers scrambled to colonize Africa, Asia, and the New World and extract the raw materials in the forms of sugar, cotton, and gold. Profitable trade routes to the mother country required protection by the nation's naval powers. A walk today in Nantes reveals how profitable this time period was, with magnificently designed eighteenth-century government and commercial buildings constructed as a result of this profitable period in which the balances of global transactions greatly favored European powers. Nantes boomed in the eighteenth century as it was the nation's largest slave-trading port. To be fair to Nantes, walks in other European cities that profited similarly from the slave trade also reveal grand buildings funded in part by human kidnapping and trafficking on a grand scale known as chattel slavery, which includes such cities as Liverpool, London, Bordeaux, Amsterdam, and Lisbon.

Of all these European cities, what makes Nantes worthy of note is a movement that commenced in the 1990s in recognizing the true human costs of this acquisition of wealth. A grassroots movement, commencing with the citizens of Nantes opposed to the idea of a national government decreeing history from above, marked the first major step to fully recognizing this part of the city's past was an exhibition: *Les Anneaux de la Memore*. Opening in 1992, the exhibition had over four hundred thousand visitors attend to learn of Nantes' role in the Atlantic slave trade. The exhibition on Nantes provided much-needed knowledge and context on the subject that had been shunned from public memory for nearly two hundred years. For example, Nantes was the largest slave port of France, with 1,714 separate slave-trading expeditions transporting more than 550,000 captive Africans to French colonies.[54]

The context from the exhibition demonstrated that it was impossible to separate the eighteenth-century economy of Nantes from the subject of slavery. The profits from this trading in human capital provided the economic steam for the entire city, affecting everyday businesses like shopkeepers, the financial sector of the city, and of course the shipbuilding industry. Additionally, the exhibition uncovered other aspects of the city's past, such as the long battle within Nantes society to eliminate the slave trade, including the ending in 1848 of the slave trade in Nantes after a successful campaign led by Victor Schoelcher.

The Memorial

In 2012, the Memorial to the Abolition of Slavery officially opened on the banks of the River Loire on the very spot where Nantes' slave ship expeditions departed on journeys south to Africa. The goal of this memorial is multiform, which is clearly stated by the mayor of Nantes Jean-marc Ayrault in a written piece called "The Memorial-Political Will." He said,

"A part of the city's wealth was therefore amassed via this odious traffic which we recognize today as a crime against humanity."[55] Of the twenty-year process of raising awareness, which commenced in the early 1990s with an exhibition and continued with the construction of the memorial and finally its dedication, Ayrault writes, "We exhumed, explored, analyzed, understood and took responsibility. This allowed us to free our conscience."[56] In this statement, it is clear this is more than just a site devoted to culpability. This is a living site not only in the struggle of human rights in the past, but also to those fighting this struggle today. Constructed as a public space to recall Nantes' past connections to slavery, the site hopes to bring awareness to the other issues of human rights that are unseen and survive in the twenty-first century. As the mayor wrote in his closing statement, "It will be a living site, a place where people unite and commit collectively to upholding the memory of past struggles and continuing our fight for the recognition and promotion of human rights."[57]

The memorial took two years to construct and covered an area of ninety thousand square feet. Designed by the award-winning Wodiczko and Bonder of Cambridge, Massachusetts, the memorial interweaves art, literature, numerous languages, geography, philosophy, and history along the waterfront. The heart of the memorial design is based on the hull of a slave ship. Descending down concert steps along the river, the viewer enters the claustrophobic extended cave-like structure, which to the left and right is ripped with concrete arch support structures on the ceilings that mirror the framing of a wooden vessel. One unique design feature is utilizing the outside wall, which is placed at an upward angle to mirror the appearance of a hull of the vessel, as an area for text. Made of etched glass, these text panels disseminate information on Nantes and her slave expeditions. Complex yet simple depending on your perspective, the site boldly utilizes glass, concert, landscaping, and vertical space. The memorial links Nantes and the human trafficking it profited from. While the link to Nantes is always central, the overall greater narrative is the global story of slavery in the three centuries of chattel slavery and its impact on the modern world we live in today. Extended along the river in the heart of town, this memorial marries artwork, structural ingenuity, and landscaping in telling a global story of human suffering and the wealth it generated. The global aspect of the memorial is of critical importance because many nations in the western hemisphere have not memorialized enforced enslavement in their national narrative. For nations like the United States that have not even attempted on a national level to come to terms with the legacy of slavery, Nantes is a critical example of dealing with a disturbing past.

Best Practices and Suggestions for Better Interpretation

- Brave action of interpreting a subject matter that has historically been shunned by societies connected to the institution of slavery.
- Demonstrates the progression of grassroots movements, starting with an investigation into the production of an exhibition flowering decades later into a public space marking the slave-trading voyages from Nantes.
- Highlights the inventive nature surrounding the creation of public space.

Conclusion

The memorialization of naval history is seen throughout societies, as this chapter has explored with examples from the continents of North America, Australasia, and Europe. All these examples link not only past to the public, but also attempt to impart the past onto the present to improve the future. For example, the *Tu Do* docked at the Australian Maritime Museum gives students a greater understanding of the lengths some of their fellow Australians went to in order to enjoy the freedoms of their society. In New Zealand, Chris Booth's sculpture memorializing the *Rainbow Warrior*, in which he utilizes the propeller from the stricken Greenpeace vessel, not only marks the attack on the nonviolent environmental organization, but also seeks to encourage bigger questions about the ship, the *Rainbow Warrior*'s mission, and why the French secret service destroyed it. Lastly, this chapter concluded with the pioneering memorial space in Nantes as a twenty-first-century attempt of coming to terms with its connections to the sixteenth through eighteenth centuries of chattel slavery.

The Memorial to the Abolition of Slavery in Nantes, as a living site, seeks to utilize a public space for the greater historical awareness of French profits of human trafficking, but also to highlight the issue of slavery today. It fully acknowledges the uncomfortable fact that slavery still exists today. As it states, "The Nantes Memorial to the abolition of slavery also has a role to play in reminding us of the dramatic urgency of the situation of slaves today."[58] Estimates today place the number of the sales of children and trafficking of young girls for prostitution at 27 million, which is a number twice as high as the total number of African slaves taken for chattel slavery in four centuries. Additionally, victims of forced migrations, debt bondage, and forced labor are estimated to be 200 million people.[59] In using the platform of a public space devoted to a naval topic, Nantes provides a prime example of interpreting history with the aim of making the citizens of a city better informed of their place in the world.

Public Memorial—Closing

On a small piece of Rhode Island coastline, a public memorial overlooks Block Island Sound. From this singular space, one can see naval history all around, with a functioning U.S. Coast Guard lighthouse half a mile away, the breakwater protecting the small fishing village with the biblical name of Galilee, and Newport some fifteen miles' distance to the east just on the horizon. Facing the south and the Atlantic surf, etched in stone is the meaning of the Point Judith Fishermen's Memorial Overlook, which states, "Dedicated in memory of those that have lost their lives at sea, and those that they leave behind."[60]

The main viewing platform for the memorial is a small bricked over area approximately twenty feet in diameter. Three stone markers stand, the center listing the title and the dedication, flanked by one inscribed with a poem titled "Sea Fever" and the other listing all individual Point Judith fishermen lost in the Atlantic. In the center of the bricked over area is a round stone bench. On the stone surface is etched a nautical compass giving the correct direction of north. One wonders if this feature was designed to give a final bearing of a direction to those lost to the waves or to the loved ones of this small New England fishing village struggling to find closure.

Behind the bricked over area, stone steps lead up fifteen feet offering a commanding view. A grassed over area with a number of stone benches grants a view of the last waters their fishermen sailed out of into Block Island Sound. From this vantage point, one sees two protective powers in the life of mariners. To the east is the Point Judith Lighthouse, with a unique two-tone design, the top half of red brick and the bottom half painted white. Built in 1857, it is the third lighthouse on the site, and is the definition of resilience in withstanding every North Atlantic storm since the U.S. Civil War.[61]

To the west is the breakwater protecting the inlet into one of the few remaining small New England towns centered economically and socially on fishing. From this memorial space, visitors witness the protective powers of this sanctuary of saltwater made possible by the manmade breakwater on the southernmost portion of Rhode Island. If you stay long enough, like those coming to this place to remember lost friends and family members do, you see and hear seagulls crying as they follow plying fishing vessels. From this point you not only mourn those lost, but also witness one of the last independently owned and operated fishing fleets in New England.

Figure 5.3.   Views of Block Island Sound from the Point Judith Fishermen's Memorial near Galilee, Rhode Island. Photo by Ben Hruska.

Memorial spaces, including statues, markers, and parks, expand and contract in meaning. Invented and constructed memorial space can remember lost individuals, vessels, and innocence of the survivors, all at the same time. The Point Judith Fishermen's Memorial Overlook exemplifies this in bringing remembrance to lost fishing vessels, fishermen, and their loved ones' pain. Looking out into Atlantic, viewers can imagine that this memorial actually expands beyond its intended design and memorializes a lost way of life. That is, this memorial marks the near closure of the New England self-sufficient fishermen that used to stretch from Maine to Connecticut that have been consumed by modernity and the global seafood industry.

Notes

1. Michael Kammen, *Mystic Chords of Memory: The Transformation of Tradition in American Culture* (New York: Knopf, 1991), 33.
2. Ibid.
3. Ibid., 104.
4. "Nuclear-Free New Zealand," New Zealand History, http://www.nzhistory.net.nz/politics/nuclear-free-new-zealand/rainbow-warrior (accessed September 3, 2015).
5. "Celebrating 30 Years of Courage," Greenpeace International, http://www.greenpeace.org/international/en/about/ships/the-rainbow-warrior/bombing-30th-anniversary (accessed September 3, 2015).
6. "Nuclear-Free New Zealand."
7. "Chris Booth Sculptor," Rainbow Warrior Memorial | Environmental artist, http://www.chrisbooth.co.nz/ethos/ (accessed September 20, 2015).
8. Ibid.
9. "Matauri Bay and the Cavalli Islands," Whangaroa, Northland New Zealand, http://www.whangaroa.co.nz/matauri-bay.cfm (accessed September 20, 2015).
10. Ibid.
11. "Rainbow Warrior," Greenpeace, http://www.rainbow-warrior.info/en/Matauri-Bay (accessed October 31, 2015).
12. Jeanne F. Brooks, "Carrier Sailors of Past Mark Dedication: Memorial on Harbor Drive Honors Seagoing Veterans," *San Diego Tribune*, September 7, 1996, 9.
13. "Naval Aircraft Carrier Memorial," from brochure of Cabrillo Lighthouse Tours of San Diego, CA, May 29, 2003, 3.
14. "Aircraft Carrier Memorial," USS *Shipley Bay*, CVE 85, http://www.shipleybay.com/memorialacc.htm (accessed February 1, 2012).
15. Brooks, "Carrier Sailors of Past Mark Dedication."
16. Ibid.
17. Ibid.
18. Ibid.
19. Fabio Gygi, "Shattered Experiences—Recycled Relics," in *Matters of Conflict: Material Vulture, Memory, and the First World War*, ed. Nickolas J. Saunders (London: Routledge, 2004), 73.
20. Ibid.

21. Efraim Sicher, "The Future of the Past: Countermemory and Postmemory in Contemporary American Post-Holocaust Narratives," *History and Memory* 12, no. 2 (2000): 70.

22. "Welcome to the Commissioning of USS George Washington, CVN 73," USS *Gambier Bay* (CVE 73), http://www.ussgambierbay-vc10.com/geoWashington.php (accessed January 26, 2012).

23. Ibid.

24. "Where Information Meets Wonder," Intrepid Sea, Air, and Space Museum Highlights Report, Fiscal years 2013 and 2014, 8.

25. Ibid.

26. Ibid., 10.

27. Ibid.

28. "Welcome Aboard: The United States Navy Memorial and Naval Heritage Center, Washington, D.C.," brochure accessed July 25, 2015, 2.

29. Informational Brochure, Commemorative Plaque Wall, The United States Navy Memorial Heritage Center, accessed by author July 25, 2015.

30. Samuel Eliot Morison, *History of United States Naval Operations in World War II Volume 10: The Atlantic Battle Won May 1943–May 1945* (Boston: Little, Brown, 1956), ix.

31. William T. Y'Blood, *Hunter-Killer: U.S. Escort Carriers in the Battle of the Atlantic* (Annapolis, MD: Naval Institute Press, 1983), vii.

32. Jane Taber, "How Halifax's Waterfront Will Honour a Historic Sea Battle on Land," *The Globe and Mail*, January 27, 2014, 8.

33. Ibid.

34. George Borgal, "HMCS Sackville: A Lady Greater Than Herself," *Action Stations!* (Winter 2015): 8–9.

35. "Our History," Australian National Maritime Museum, http://www.anmm.gov.au/About-Us/Our-History (accessed September 29, 2015).

36. "What We Do," Australian National Maritime Museum, http://www.anmm.gov.au/about-us/what-we-do (accessed September 29, 2015).

37. "Tu Do: A Boat Called Freedom," Australian National Maritime Museum, http://www.anmm.gov.au/whats-on/vessels/tu-do (accessed September 29, 2015).

38. "Our People," Australia.gov.au, http://www.australia.gov.au/about-australia/our-country/our-people (accessed September 29, 2015).

39. "Tu Do: A Boat Called Freedom."

40. "Immigration: School Excursion Program," Australian National Maritime Museum, http://www.anmm.gov.au/Learn/School-Excursions/Immigration (accessed September 30, 2015).

41. "Charles W. Morgan," Mystic Seaport Museum, http//:www.mysticseaport.org/visit/explore/morgan/ (accessed October 8, 2015).

42. "About Mystic Seaport," Mystic Seaport Museum, http://www.mysticseaport.org/about/ (accessed October 16, 2015).

43. Ibid.

44. "Whaleship Charles W. Morgan Arrives to Warm Welcome," *Vineyard Gazette*, http://vineyardgazette.com/news/2014/06/19/whaleship-charles-w-morgan-arrives-warm-welcome?k=vg5622b276b14f1&r=1 (accessed October 17, 2015).

45. "Voyaging in the Wake of the Whalers," Mystic Seaport Museum, http://www.mysticseaport.org/locations/exhibits/voyaging-in-the-wake-of-the-whalers/ (accessed October 18, 2015).

46. Ibid.

47. Ibid.

48. "History of the Naval Memorial," The German Naval Memorial, http://www.deutscher-marinebund.de/geschichte_me_english.htm (accessed October 19, 2015).

49. Ibid.

50. Ibid.

51. Ibid.

52. Ibid.

53. Ibid.

54. "Nantes Facing Up to Its History," Memorial to the Abolition of Slavery, http://memorial.nantes.fr/en/le-memorial/nantes-face-a-son-histoire (accessed November 1, 2015).

55. "The Memorial: Political Will," Memorial to the Abolition of Slavery, http://memorial.nantes.fr/en/le-memorial/une-volonte-politique (accessed November 1, 2015).

56. Ibid.

57. Ibid.

58. "Slavery Today," Memorial to the Abolition of Slavery, http://memorial.nantes.fr/en/esclavage-et-lutte-pour-la-liberte/l'esclavage-aujourd'hui (accessed November 1, 2015).

59. Ibid.

60. "New Home," Point Judith Fishermen's Memorial Foundation, http://pjfmf.org (accessed January 3, 2016).

61. "Point Judith, RI," Lighthouse Friends, http://www.lighthousefriends.com/light.asp?ID=400 (accessed August 15, 2015).

CHAPTER 6

Entering Port

Conclusion

ACCORDING TO A U.S. DEPARTMENT of Defense 2012 fiscal year report, eighty-seven national museums exist dedicated to honor the American military. The U.S. Army lays claim to the vast majority with fifty-six museums, the U.S. Air Force has thirteen, the U.S. Navy has eleven, and the U.S. Marine Corps has just five. In addition, two other defense agencies operate the remaining two museums. This leaves the U.S. Coast Guard, with a history stretching back two hundred years, with no official location for interpretation, exhibition, or preservation.[1] However, a national effort is underway to construct a new National Coast Guard Museum, on the harbor of New London, Connecticut. The main theme of the fifty-four-thousand-square-foot building will be the Coast Guard's motto, *Semper Paratus* (Always Ready).

The museum, which will open in 2018, demonstrates in two ways successful long-range planning of maritime museums.[2] First, the proposed operational methodology of the site includes a mixture of permanent and revolving exhibitions using interactive technology to engage both Coast Guard veterans and the general public. At the same time, however, understanding the power of objects, a Coast Guard helicopter will rest on the roof of the four-story structure. Using a holistic approach in blending both place and space, visitors will see the dangerous juncture where land meets sea from this open-air platform. From the museum roof, visitors will look out at a historic juncture in American maritime history, the point where the Thames River and the Atlantic Ocean merge into one.

This last point foreshadows the second successful theme, that of heritage tourism. The National Trust of Historic Preservation defines heritage tourism as "traveling to experience the places, artifacts and activities that authentically represent the stories and people of the past."[3] Sites to attract visitors can be of cultural, historic, and natural resources, and, in a perfect situation, would include all three. This concept is much bigger than just one large museum. Heritage tourism is a much greater goal, and like any large objective, requires coordination and planning in lining up like-minded cultural organizations in transforming their surrounding community in a positive way. Beyond simply trying to impact the visitor inside a museum's walls, which is a very noble goal, heritage tourism sees a museum working in a partnership with other entities seeking to transform the economic and social environs. The end goal is giving an economic benefit for cultural organizations and for-profit businesses in a given area to improve the quality of life for visitors and the residents by embracing their heritage and culture.

Currently, New London is at a crossroads. Exiting the train station, one sees a historic downtown with stone buildings from the mid-nineteenth century. The downtown is far from a slum; however, it is not the most inviting environment. While some buildings house neighborhood restaurants and businesses, about half of the buildings are empty with for rent signs hanging in street-facing windows. For the thousands that travel just to the north on Interstate 95, few purposefully exit to visit the current state of the waterfront on the west side of the Thames River. However, the potential for molding the cultural and historic elements into a coherent theme and allowing gravity to coalesce around a consortium of cultural institutions and businesses in attracting visitors, as opposed to just the limited few competing with one another for the handful that currently visit, is huge.

The foundational heritage exists. Just down the street from the Amtrak station is the Custom House Maritime Museum. While the upstairs houses the oldest U.S. Custom Office in the nation, the rest of the building has been devoted to interpreting the maritime history of New London. Most notable among these is New London being the location where the African slaves who revolted and took over the nineteenth-century two-masted schooner *La Amistad* were turned in to U.S. government authorities after they entered the jurisdiction of the United States. From the *Amistad* exhibition on the second floor one can look to the waterfront to the south and see a reconstructed *La Amistad* built in the year 2000 and now docked and on display. In addition, the greater governing entity of the museum is the New England Maritime Society, which oversees and preserves three historic lighthouses.[4]

In an open park area outside the train station stands a fifty-foot-tall granite obelisk titled "Soldiers' and Sailors' Monument," which is unique for Civil War memorials as it marks the naval war as well as the battles fought on land. Just upriver on the banks of the Thames River is the U.S. Coast Guard Academy. Across the river from New London is Groton, the submarine capital of the world, and the New London waterfront overlooks the General Dynamics assembly area that pieces together the future submarines of the U.S. Navy. Lastly, along the waterfront stands a sign giving notice to the future location of the National Coast Guard Museum. Maritime history is rich and powerful enough to make New London a destination for art, history, cultural, and seaside environments as well as strong enough to remake the downtown area. A sharp increase in visitation would allow for not only the maritime museums to prosper, but also for the vacant historic buildings to be rehabbed and help revitalize a New England seaside community rich in maritime history.

Figure 6.1. On the waterfront in New London, Connecticut, the future home of the National Coast Guard Museum. Photo by Ben Hruska.

The beginning stages of such a movement are seen in Connecticut by the Sea, a partnership of the Florence Griswold Museum, the Connecticut River Museum, and the New London Custom House Maritime Museum. Stressing three themes of art, history, and adventure, all viewed through the maritime lens, these three sites offer packaging of admission. Together, these three museums invite visitors to climb and learn on board a replica of the *Turtle*, a submarine used during the American Revolution, or learn that man's relationship with the Connecticut River extends back through centuries of the tribal history of the Mohegan and Pequot tribes. Other options include cooking classes of local seafood or taking a boat ride across Long Island Sound to visit a lighthouse on an isolated rock island.[5] Nearly all experiences represent a major shift in celebrating maritime culture from the model utilized in the early twentieth century.

In 1922, the nation of Britain, whose history is impossible to separate into naval and nonnaval themes, saved a ship of war by transforming it into a memorial. Placed in dry dock, the HMS *Victory* in Portsmouth, England, was turned into a near place of worship to see the location where Lord Horatio Nelson, one of the nation's fallen heroes, fell on this deck in the battle of Trafalgar in 1805. A century later, this one-dimensional approach to naval interpretation, no matter how successful, is no longer viable. The best hope with regard to the twenty-first-century model of success with heritage tourism is a wide range of institutions and for-profit businesses coalescing around a historical theme. That being said, that is why this author has faith in the New London plan formulating heritage tourism with a naval theme to take root.

Beyond the above-mentioned New London museums, future plans are in the works including a walking trail modeled after Boston's Freedom Trail. This trail weaving through the streets of Boston, which starts at the Boston Common and ends across the Charles River near Bunker Hill, is one of the most successful models of independent sites coming together to tell a common story. The proposed trail would highlight the naval history of both New London and Groton, and keeping with the maritime theme, walkers would traverse the Thames River that divides the two communities on small motor launches.[6] Thus, walkers would experience both sides by the means from which they sprang, as residents and commerce first arrived in Connecticut seaside towns by water and not by modern-day rivers of asphalt.

The assemblage of New London and Groton historical organizations vary in size, scope, and mission, thus serving as a microcosm of the interpretive techniques employed by museums. All are blessed with the living and still ongoing naval traditions around them with the construction of submarines by General Dynamics in Groton and the education at the U.S. Coast Guard Academy just up the Thames River. However, modernity has transformed naval and maritime traditions, and early generations of remembering the sea in the twentieth century are slipping away from living memory and in need of protection and recording before this generation of mariners passes away. Man's relationship with the sea is very much alive where the Thames River enters the Long Island Sound. Thus, interpreting naval history as an ongoing process, still very much relative and visible on the New London waterfront, allowing museum interpretation to coalesce around a big tent approach to community programs. Teaming up with one another, embracing art, food, and cultural aspects, and the forthcoming National Coast Guard Museum on the waterfront, New London will be an example of heritage tourism that all museum professionals of naval exhibitions will want to watch closely.

"Sea Blindness"

For the average American today it is very easy to be completely oblivious to the importance of naval power and the oceans in shaping our daily lives. Even the most informed members of our society, who devour all sections of a range of Sunday newspapers, are nearly completely ignorant of the oceans' political, economic, and social ramifications. This is not only in the United States, with our oftentimes America-centric world outlook, because this is ignorance on the global level. In fact, it even has a term, *sea blindness*. The Atlantic Council, an organization devoted to providing a platform for understanding the rapidly changing twenty-first century and whose bipartisan honorary directors includes former Secretaries of State Madeleine K. Albright and Condoleezza Rice, describes this as "an inability to appreciate the central role the oceans and naval power have played in securing our strategic security and economic prosperity."[7]

One recent author, Rose George, has written about the invisible industry of global shipping by taking a five-week journey over nine thousand nautical miles from southern England to Singapore. Her research trip, where she sailed with the crew mostly composed of Filipinos, allowed her to experience firsthand the importance of global shipping today and also the Spartan lifestyle of the crew. As the *New York Times* book review correctly noted, this is a moral tale to give voice to workers overlooked by both transnational shipping corporations and human watch groups. As she quips, "Buy your fair-trade coffee beans by all means, but don't assume fair-trade principles govern the conditions of the men who fetch it to you. You would be mistaken."[8]

In her work *Ninety Percent of Everything: Inside Shipping, the Invisible Industry That Puts Clothes on Your Back, Gas in Your Car, and Food on Your Plate*, George weaves tales blending global statistics with the human experiences of the crew, the very goal of many of us in public programs and exhibitions. Conditions on modern-day container vessels differ very little from a sweatshop, with poor food, no Internet or cell phone use for weeks, and no information on what they are hauling. She makes the reader rethink the global impact their purchases incur on social, environmental, and humanitarian issues. When possible, she includes facts that boggle the mind, such as, "Shipping is so cheap that it makes financial sense for Scottish cod to be sent 10,000 miles to China to be filleted, then sent back to Scottish shops and restaurants, than to pay Scottish filleters."[9]

All these concepts, which serve to make visitors rethink their environment, to ask questions about their consumption, and to give voice to the voiceless, embody the center pillars of public historians. The oceans are still deadly. Even today, on average two ships are lost a week, which claims two thousand seafarers a year. Does anyone filling their gas tank, brewing coffee, or using their electronics think of these unseen ocean crossings or the men who make these possible? The current relationship with man and the ocean is unknown to the general public and thus invisible, meaning we as practitioners of naval/maritime heritage manage fertile ground full of potential.

Additionally, the average American does not have a direct connection to the U.S. Navy. When compared to the numbers of sailors in the twentieth century, both during World War II and the duration of the Cold War, the size of the U.S. Navy today is very small. So small, in fact, it is rare for the average citizen to know someone on active duty when compared to the previous century. Currently, the U.S. Navy has 326,612 active duty sailors and 273 deployable battle force ships.[10] While this may seem incredibly small compared to the peak of 1945 in World War II, where these numbers were over three million sailors and six thousand vessels,[11] the amount of firepower gained with technologies such as nuclear propulsion, Polaris submarines armed with nuclear weapons, and jet aircraft is difficult to overstate. In case of humanitarian crisis or outbreak of war, the U.S. Navy is more than capable of protecting the interests of the United States.

Naval history is beyond relevant. In 2016, the first of the next generation of U.S. Navy aircraft carriers will come on line. With one hundred thousand tons of displacement, a cost of $13 billion, and a projected service life of fifty years, the USS *Gerald R. Ford*, CVN-78, will be the home of U.S. Navy sailors yet unborn.[12] As the geopolitical implications of the emerging economies in Asia, such as India and China, remain to be seen, understanding our naval past as a nation and a species is of critical significance. Whether our products of history and remembrance seek to bring relevance to our military past or to our position in the twenty-first-century economy, we all seek to cultivate topics relevant to a range of potential visitors.

Coda

In July 2015, one of the leading newspapers in India ran a short article. *The Tribune* reported on the world's longest-serving aircraft carrier, the INS *Viraat*, R 22, which was scheduled for decommission in 2016 and the Indian government already had plans to convert her into a floating museum. In addition, $3 million (U.S.) of the Indian government funds had been allocated for the project, eliminating any need for fundraising with private donations.[13] The carrier's fifty-seven-year-long career began in Britain's Royal Navy when she was commissioned in 1959 as the HMS *Hermes*, R 12. In 1982, she served as the flagship of naval presence of the Royal Navy in the South Atlantic in the Falkland Islands War. India purchased her in 1986, and she officially joined her Navy the following year. By this time, she had been converted for the Harrier vertical/short takeoff jump jet and outfitted with a "ski jump" at the bow of the vessel, adding to her unique appearance.[14] While India will not be leaving the club of carrier aviation with the retiring of the *Viraat*, the national government has embraced preserving and protecting its symbol of naval power by converting it into a floating museum. This museum, like war vessels themselves, will be designed in a compartmentalized fashion to complete a number of missions at the same time, whether these project national power or preserve heritage.

Notes

1. "National Coast Guard Museum," Brochure, National Coast Guard Museum Association, Inc. (accessed July 2015).

2. "National Coast Guard Museum Association, Opening 2018," Brochure, National Coast Guard Museum Association, Inc. (accessed July 2015).

3. "Heritage Tourism," National Trust for Historic Preservation, http://www.preservation-nation.org/information-center/economics-of-revitalization/heritage-tourism (accessed August 6, 2015).

4. "Maritimes, Custom House," Brochure, Fifth Annual Sentinels of the Sound, Summer 2015, New London Custom House Maritime Museum (accessed July 2015).

5. "Art-History-Adventure," Brochure, Connecticut and the Sea (accessed July 2015).

6. Ibid.

7. "Ending America's 'Sea Blindness,'" Atlantic Council, http://www.atlanticcouncil.org/blogs/new-atlanticist/ending-americas-sea-blindness (accessed August 9, 2015).

8. "Life on Ships That Make World Go Round," review of *Ninety Percent of Everything* by Rose George, *New York Times*, http://www.nytimes.com/2013/10/17/books/ninety-percent-of-everything-by-rose-george.html?_r=0 (accessed August 10, 2015).

9. Ibid.

10. "Status of the Navy," America's Navy, http://www.navy.mil/navydata/nav_legacy.asp?id=146 (accessed August 11, 2015).

11. "By the Numbers," The National World War II Museum, http://www.nationalww2museum.org/learn/education/for-students/ww2-history/ww2-by-the-numbers/us-military.html (accessed August 11, 2015).

12. "Design: Ready for the 21st Century," Gerald R. Ford (CVN 78), http://thefordclass.com/design.html (accessed August 10, 2015).

13. "INS Viraat to Turn into a Museum," The Tribune, http://www.tribuneindia.com/news/nation/ins-viraat-to-turn-into-a-museum/102073.html (accessed August 18, 2015).

14. "World's Oldest Active Aircraft Carrier INS Viraat Set to Be Museum Ship in India," USNI News, http://news.usni.org/2015/07/06/worlds-oldest-active-aircraft-carrier-ins-viraat-set-to-be-museum-ship-in-india (accessed August 18, 2015).

Bibliography

Alexander, Aimee. "Forever a Merchant Marine." *Tampa Bay Times*, December 22, 2013.

All Hands. "The Big Ben Comes Home." June 1945. Number 339.

Amato, Joseph A. *Guilt and Gratitude: A Study of the Origins of Contemporary Conscience.* London: Greenwood Press, 1982.

———. *Jacob's Well: A Case for Rethinking Family History.* St. Paul, MN: Minnesota Historical Society Press, 2008.

———. *Rethinking Home: A Case for Writing Local History.* Berkeley: University of California Press, 2002.

American Association for State and Local History. "Vashon Island's Native People." AASLH Awards, http://awards.aaslh.org/award/vashon-islands-native-people-navigating-seas-of-change (accessed January 15, 2015).

American Victory Ship Mariners Museum. Pamphlet: An American Icon and National Treasure. Tampa, Florida (accessed December 20, 2015).

———. "Welcome Aboard." http://www.americanvictory.org (accessed December 23, 2015).

America's Navy. "Carriers: The List." http://www.navy.mil/navydata/ships/carriers/cv-list.asp (accessed January 11, 2016).

———. "Fact File: Aircraft Carriers." http://www.navy.mil/navydata/fact_display.asp?cid=4200&tid=200&ct=4 (accessed January 11, 2016).

———. "Status of the Navy." http://www.navy.mil/navydata/nav_legacy.asp?id=146 (accessed August 11, 2015).

Arizona State Capital Museum. USS *Arizona* exhibition panel, Phoenix, Arizona. Visited by author April 3, 2015.

Arizona State Library Archives and Public Records. "Exhibits." http://www.azlibrary.gov/azcm/exhibits (accessed May 30, 2015).

"Army & Navy." *Time*, October 29, 1945.

Atlantic Council. "Ending America's 'Sea Blindness.'" http://www.atlanticcouncil.org/blogs/new-atlanticist/ending-americas-sea-blindness (accessed August 9, 2015).

Australia.gov.au. "Our People." http://www.australia.gov.au/about-australia/our-country/our-people (accessed September 29, 2015).

Australian National Maritime Museum. "Immigration: School Excursion Program." http://www.anmm.gov.au/Learn/School-Excursions/Immigration (accessed September 30, 2015).

———. "Our History." http://www.anmm.gov.au/About-Us/Our-History (accessed September 29, 2015).

———. "Tu Do: A Boat Called Freedom." http://www.anmm.gov.au/whats-on/vessels/tu-do (accessed September 29, 2015).

———. "What We Do." http://www.anmm.gov.au/about-us/what-we-do (accessed September 29, 2015).

Ayres Jr., B. Drummond. "Carrier Kennedy Is Handed Over to Navy by Caroline." *New York Times*, September 8, 1968.

Ballard, Chris. "The Ship as Symbol in the Prehistory of Scandinavia and Southeast Asia." *World Archeology* 35, no. 3 (2003): 385–403.

Battleship Cove Celebrating 50 Years. "Nautical Nights Overnight Program." http://www.battleshipcove.org/nautical-nights (accessed August 27, 2015).

Battleship Mikasa. "A Living Naval Museum." http://aroundtokyo.net/blog/2012/10/28/battleship-mikasa (accessed November 9, 2015).

Beidler, Philip D. *The Good War's Greatest Hits: World War II and American Remembering*. Athens: University of Georgia Press, 1998.

Bodnar, John. *Remaking of America: Public Memory, Commemoration, and Patriotism in the Twentieth Century*. Princeton, NJ: Princeton University Press, 1992.

Boot, Max. *The Savage Wars of Peace: Small Wars and the Rise of American Power*. New York: Basic Books, 2002.

Borgal, George. "HMCS Sackville: A Lady Greater Than Herself." *Actions Stations!* (Winter 2015).

Black, Shameem. "Commemoration from a Distance: On Metamemorial Fiction." *History and Memory* 23, no. 2 (2011): 40–65.

Block Island Historical Society. USS Block Island Collection. Document Number 06.74.01. Block Island, Rhode Island.

———. USS Block Island Collection. Object Number 06.05.2005. Block Island, Rhode Island.

———. USS Block Island Collection. Object Number 06.10.2007. Block Island, Rhode Island.

———. USS Block Island Collection. Object Number 06.12.2007. Block Island, Rhode Island.

BBC History. "Battle of Trafalgar." http://www.bbc.co.uk/history/british/empire_seapower/trafalgar_01.shtml#six (accessed November 30, 2015).

Brooks, Jeanne F. "Carrier Sailors of Past Mark Dedication: Memorial on Harbor Drive Honors Seagoing Veterans." *San Diego Tribune*, September 7, 1996.

Bullock Museum. "La Belle: The Ship That Changed History." http://www.thestoryoftexas.com/la-belle/the-exhibit (accessed September 2, 2015).

———. "Press Information." http://www.thestoryoftexas.com/about/press (accessed September 2, 2015).

Buschmann, Rainer F. *Oceans in World History*. Boston: McGraw Hill Higher Education, 2007.

Cabrillo Lighthouse Tours. "Naval Aircraft Carrier Memorial." Brochure dated May 29, 2003. San Diego, CA.

Canby, Vincent. "On Film, the Battle of 'Midway' is Lost." *New York Times*, June 19, 1976.

Center of Association Leadership. "Associations Now." https://www.asaecenter.org/Resources/ANowDetail.cfm?ItemNumber=46320 (accessed January 5, 2016).

Chicago Department of Aviation. "Battle of Midway Heroes Honored a Chicago Midway Airport." http://www.ohare.com/About/Midway/BattleOfMidway.aspx (accessed October 14, 2011).

———. "History of O'Hare International Airport." http://www.ohare.com/About/History/Default.aspx (accessed October 14, 2011).

Clark, David. "Museum Ship Exhibits: There and Back Again." Self-published and given to the author on April 3, 2014.

———. "Traditional Museums vs. Ship Museums." Self-published and given to the author on April 3, 2014.

Classic Country Lyrics. "Okie From Muskogee." http://www.classic-country-song-lyrics.com/okiefrommuskogeelyricschords.html (accessed January 9, 2016).

CNN News. "HMS Victory: World's Oldest Warship to get $25 Facelift." http://www.cnn.com/2011/12/05/world/europe/hms-victory (accessed December 3, 2015).

Connecticut and the Sea. "Art-History-Adventure." Brochure. New London, Connecticut (accessed July 2015).

Cross, Wilbur. *Naval Battles and Heroes*. New York: Perennial Library, 1960.

Dawn. "Karachi: Submarine Hangor on Display in Museum." http://www.dawn.com/news/279766/karachi-submarine-hangor-on-display-in-museum (accessed December 13, 2015).

Department of Defense. Memorandum from the Department of the Navy. "*Lexington* to *Cnaira*." Corpus Christi, Texas. December 19, 1974.

Detroit Historical Society. "Built By the River." http://detroithistorical.org/dossin-great-lakes-museum/exhibitions/signature-exhibitions/built-river (accessed January 11, 2016).

Donovan, Robert J. *PT 109: John F. Kennedy in World War II*. Fawcett Publications, 1961.

Downie, Robert M. "Block Island's Pair of Aircraft Carriers." *Providence Journal*, May 15, 1989.

Durel, John and Anita. "A Golden Age for Historic Properties." *History News*, Summer 2007.

Escort Carrier Sailors and Airmen Association. "ESCAA Museum Information." http://escort-carriers.com/museums.html (accessed February 1, 2012).

———. "Escort Carrier Display." http://www.escortcarriers.com/museums.html (accessed December 7, 2011).

Eliade, Mircea. *Cosmos and History: The Myth of the Eternal Return*. New York: Harper and Row, 1959.

Explore St. Paul's Cathedral. "The Tomb of Lord Nelson (1758–1805)." http://www.explore-st-pauls.net/oct03/textMM/NelsonTombN.htm (accessed November 30, 2015).

Falgout, Suzanne, Lin Poyer, and Laurence M. Carucci. *Memories of War: Micronesians in the Pacific War*. Honolulu: University of Hawaii Press, 2008.

Feinberg, Alexander. "Mighty Carrier Roosevelt Commissioned by Truman." *New York Times*, October 28, 1945.

First Peoples Worldwide. "About Us." http://www.firstpeoples.org/about-us/about-us (accessed January 21, 2016).

Forbes. "The Silo Mentality." http://www.forbes.com/sites/brentgleeson/2013/10/02/the-silo-mentality-how-to-break-down-the-barriers (accessed January 6, 2016).

Frankel, Max. "Family of Late President and Johnson at Ceremony." *New York Times*, May 28, 1967.

Garner, Dwight. "Life on Ships That Make World Go Round." Review of *Ninety Percent of Everything*, by Rose George. *New York Times*, August 10, 2015. http://www.nytimes.com/2013/10/17/books/ninety-percent-of-everything-by-rose-george.html?_r=0.

Gerald R. Ford (CVN 78). "Design: Ready for the 21st Century." http://thefordclass.com/design.html (accessed August 10, 2015).

German Naval Memorial. "History of the Naval Memorial." http://www.deutscher-marinebund.de/geschichte_me_english.htm (accessed October 19, 2015).

Gibbings, Beth. "Remembering the SIEV X: Who Care for the Bodies of the Stateless, Lost at Sea?" *The Public Historian* 32, no. 1 (2010): 13–30.

Greenpeace. "Rainbow Warrior." http://www.rainbow-warrior.info/en/Matauri-Bay (accessed October 31, 2015).

Greenpeace International. "Celebrating 30 Years of Courage." http://www.greenpeace.org/international/en/about/ships/the-rainbow-warrior/bombing-30th-anniversary (accessed September 3, 2015).

Guardian. "North Korea to Put US Spy Ship Captured in 1968 on Display." http://www.theguardian.com/world/2013/jul/25/north-korea-us-spy-ship-museum (accessed December 13, 2015).

Gygi, Fabio. "Shattered Experiences—Recycled Relics." In *Matters of Conflict: Material Culture, Memory and the First World War*, edited by Nicholas J. Saunders. New York: Routledge, 2004.

Hass, Kristin Ann. *Carried to the Wall: American Memory and the Vietnam Veterans Memorial*. Berkeley: University of California Press, 1998.

Historical Marker Database. "Arizona's U.S.S. Arizona Memorial." http://www.hmdb.org/marker.asp?marker=26425 (accessed May 30, 2015).

HMS Victory: National Museum of the Royal Navy. "Restoration." http://www.hms-victory.com/restoration (accessed December 1, 2015).

Hornfischer, James D. *The Last Stand of the Tin Can Sailors: The Extraordinary World War II Story of the U.S. Navy's Finest Hour*. New York: Random House, 2004.

Intrepid.org. "'Kamikaze: Day of Darkness' Exhibit Returns." Press Releases. http://www.intrepidmuseum.org/About-Us/Press-Room/Press-Releases/"KAMIKAZE--DAY-OF-DARKNESS,-DAY-OF-LIGHT"-EXHIBIT-.aspx (accessed August 17, 2015).

Intrepid Sea and Space Museum Highlights Report. "Where Information Meets Wonder." Fiscal years 2013 and 2014.

John F. Kennedy Presidential Library and Museum. "Remarks at O'Hare International Airport Dedication, Chicago, Illinois, 23 March 1963." http://www.jfklibrary.org/Asset-Viewer/Archives/JFKPOF-043-024.aspx (accessed October 14, 2011).

Kammen, Michael. *Mystic Chords of Memory: The Transformation of Tradition in American Culture*. New York: Knopf, 1991.

Keegan, John. *The Battle for History: Re-Fighting World War II*. New York: Vintage Books, 1995.

Kennedy, Maxwell Taylor. *Danger's Hour: The Story of the USS Bunker Hill and the Kamikaze Pilot Who Crippled Her*. New York: Simon and Schuster, 2008.

Klein, Bernhard, and Gesa Mankenthum, eds. *Sea Changes: Historicizing the Ocean*. New York: Routledge, 2004.

Kure Maritime Museum. "Yamato." http://yamatomuseum.com (accessed November 8, 2015).

LaCapra, Dominick. *History and Memory After Auschwitz*. Ithaca, NY: Cornell University Press, 1998.

Landsberg, Alison. *Prosthetic Memory: The Transformation of American Remembrance in the Age of Mass Culture*. New York: Columbia University Press, 2004.

Lawson, Ted W. *Thirty Seconds Over Tokyo*. Dulles, VA: Brassey's Inc., 1943.

LeRoy, Mervyn. *Thirty Seconds Over Tokyo*. DVD. First released 1944. Los Angeles: Metro-Gold-wyn-Mayer, 1999.

Lighthouse Friends. "Point Judith, RI." http://www.lighthousefriends.com/light.asp?ID=400 (accessed August 15, 2015).

Londontopia. "10 Random Facts and Figures about Trafalgar Square." http://londontopia.net/guides/10-random-facts-and-figures-about-trafalgar-square (accessed November 30, 2015).

Lundstrom, John B. *Fateful Rendezvous: The Life of Butch O'Hare*. Annapolis: Naval Institute Press, 1997.

Macchia, Joe. Interviewed by Ben Hruska, October 17, 2011, Tempe, Arizona.

MacInnes, Bill, ed. *Chips Off the Old Block* 1 (1983).

———. *Chips Off the Old Block* 4 (1983).

———. *Chips Off the Old Block* 3 (1985).

———. *Chips Off the Old Block* 3 (1986).

———. *Chips Off the Old Block* 1 (2004).

———. *Chips Off the Old Block* 1 (2006).

———. *Chips Off the Old Block* 3 (2006).

———. Email message to the author, June 12, 2011.

———. Email message to the author, June 26, 2011.

Marrow, Lance. *The Best Year of Their Lives: Kennedy, Johnson, and Nixon in 1948*. New York: Basic Books, 2005.

McKinnon, Shaun. "'We Have to Remember': A Date Which Will Live in Infamy." *Arizona Republic*, December 7, 2015.

Memorial to the Abolition of Slavery. "Nantes Facing Up to Its History." http://memorial.nantes.fr/en/le-memorial/nantes-face-a-son-histoire (accessed November 1, 2015).

———. "Slavery Today." http://memorial.nantes.fr/en/esclavage-et-lutte-pour-la-liberte/l'esclavage-aujourd'hui (accessed November 1, 2015).

———. "The Memorial: Political Will." http://memorial.nantes.fr/en/le-memorial/une-volonte-politique (accessed November 1, 2015).

Morison, Samuel Eliot. *History of United States Naval Operations in World War II Volume 10: The Atlantic Battle Won May 1943–May 1945*. Boston: Little, Brown, 1956.

———. *History of United States Naval Operations in World War II Volume 12: Leyte, June 1944–January 1945*. Boston: Little, Brown, 1963.

Muskogee War Memorial Park. "Home of the USS Batfish." http://warmemorialpark.org (accessed November 29, 2015).

Mystic Seaport Museum. "About Mystic Seaport." http://www.mysticseaport.org/about (accessed October 16, 2015).

———. "Charles W. Morgan." http//:www.mysticseaport.org/visit/explore/morgan (accessed October 8, 2015).

———. "Voyaging in the Wake of the Whalers." http://www.mysticseaport.org/locations/exhibits/voyaging-in-the-wake-of-the-whalers (accessed October 18, 2015).

"National Affairs." *Time*, November 5, 1945.

National Coast Guard Museum Association, Inc. "National Coast Guard Museum." Brochure. New London, Connecticut (accessed July 2015).

———. "National Coast Guard Museum Association, Opening 2018." Brochure. New London, Connecticut (accessed July 2015).

National Museum of the Pacific War. "Home." http://www.pacificwarmuseum.org/Index.asp (accessed February 7, 2012).

———. "Search Memorial Plaques." http://www.pacificwarmuseum.org/SearchPlaques.asp?LastLetter=l (accessed February 7, 2012).

National Naval Aviation Museum. "Aircraft and Exhibits." http://www.navalaviationmuseum.org/attractions/aircraft-exhibits (accessed August 25, 2015).

National Park Service. Liberty Ships and Victory Ships. "Determining the Facts." http://www.nps.gov/nr/twhp/wwwlps/lessons/116liberty_victory_ships/116facts2.htm (accessed December 27, 2015).

———. World War II Valor in the Pacific National Monument. "History and Culture." http://www.nps.gov/valr/learn/historyculture/index.htm (accessed November 11, 2015).

National Trust for Historic Preservation. "Heritage Tourism." http://www.preservationnation.org/information-center/economics-of-revitalization/heritage-tourism (accessed August 6, 2015).

National World War II Museum in New Orleans. "By the Numbers." http://www.nationalww-2museum.org/learn/education/for-students/ww2-history/ww2-by-the-numbers/us-military.html (accessed August 11, 2015).

Naval History and Heritage Command. "Long Island II (CVE-1)." http://www.history.navy.mil/research/histories/ship-histories/danfs/l/long-island-ii.html (accessed August 12, 2015).

———. "Re-Internment of John Paul Jones." http://www.theodore-roosevelt.com/images/research/speeches/trjpjburial.pdf (accessed January 9, 2016).

———. "Ship's Bells." http://www.history.navy.mil/faqs/faq83-1.htm (accessed May 18, 2011).

———. "USS Intrepid (CV-11)." http://www.history.navy.mil/our-collections/photography/us-navy-ships/aircraft-carriers/uss-intrepid--cv-11-.html (accessed August 21, 2015).

New London Custom House Maritime Museum. "Maritimes, Custom House." Brochure. Fifth Annual Sentinels of the Sound, Summer 2015. New London, Connecticut (accessed July 2015).

———. "Naval Toys Exhibition." Visited by author July 21, 2015. New London, Connecticut.

New Zealand History. "Nuclear-Free New Zealand." http://www.nzhistory.net.nz/politics/nuclear-free-new-zealand/rainbow-warrior (accessed September 3, 2015).

Nora, Pierre. "Between Memory and History: Les Lieux de Memoire." *Representations* no. 26 (1989): 7–24.

NOVA: Building Pharaoh's Ship. "Exploring the Pharaoh's Boat." http://www.pbs.org/wgbh/nova/pharaoh/expl-nf.html (accessed December 10, 2015).

Oakland Museum of California. "Exhibition." http://museumca.org/exhibit/above-and-below-stories-our-changing-bay?qt-above_and_below=0#qt-above_and_below (accessed January 6, 2016).

Pakistan Affairs. "We Sank the Khukri." http://www.pakistanaffairs.pk/threads/9540-INS-Khuk-ri-was-sunk-by-PNS-HANGOR-on-9-Dec-1971-41-yrs-back/page2 (accessed December 13, 2015).

Patriot's Point Home of the USS Yorktown. "Hands-On History Lesson." http://www.patriotspoint.org/explore_museum (accessed August 28, 2015).

Pima Air and Space Museum. Freshwater Aircraft Carriers exhibition panel. Tucson, Arizona. Visited by the author, November 11, 2015.

———. Nose Art and Insignia: Beyond the Girls exhibition panel. Tucson, Arizona. Visited by the author, November 11, 2015.

Point Judith Fishermen's Memorial Foundation. "New Home." http://pjfmf.org (accessed January 3, 2016).

Polmar, Norman. *Aircraft Carriers: A Graphic History of Carrier Aviation and Its Influence on World Events.* Garden City, NY: Doubleday, 1969.

Potochniak, Tony. *Return to the Philippines.* USS *Gambier Bay* Association, 2005.

PR Newswire. "Battleship Cove Launches Dynamic New Exhibit Reenacting the Attack on Pearl Harbor." http://www.prnewswire.com/news-releases/battleship-cove-launches-dynamic-new-exhibit-reenacting-the-attack-on-pearl-harbor-127509663.html (accessed May 21, 2015).

Pratt, Fletcher. *The Navy's War.* New York: Harper and Brothers Publishers, 1943.

Pyne, Stephen. *Voyager: Seeking Newer Worlds in the Third Great Age of Discovery.* New York: Viking Press, 2010.

Rainbow Warrior Memorial | Environmental artist. 'Chris Booth Sculptor." http://www.chris-booth.co.nz/ethos (accessed September 20, 2015).

Russia Beyond the Headlines. "Aurora: The Cruiser that Sparked a Revolution—Or Did It?" http://rbth.com/arts/2014/11/07/aurora_the_cruiser_that_sparked_a_revolution_or_did_it_41229.html (accessed December 12, 2015).

Saunders, Nicholas J. "Material Culture and Conflict: The Great War, 1914–2003." In *Matters of Conflict: Material Culture, Memory and the First World War*, edited by Nicholas J. Saunders, 5–25. New York: Routledge, 2004.

Seacoast New Hampshire. "The Two Burials of John Paul Jones." http://www.seacoastnh.com/jpj/burial.html (accessed January 9, 2016).

Ship Modeling Mailing List. "CVE-9 Bogue USN Escort Carrier: Tamiya 1/700." http://smmlonline.com/reviews/models/bogue/bogue.html (accessed December 7, 2011).

Sicher, Efraim. "The Future of the Past: Countermemory and Postmemory in Contemporary American Post-Holocaust Narratives." *History and Memory* 12, no. 2 (2000): 56–91.

Smight, Jack. *Midway.* DVD. Frist released in 1976. Los Angeles: Universal, 1996.

Suid, Lawrence H. *Sailing the Silver Screen: Hollywood and the U.S. Navy.* Annapolis: Naval Institute Press, 1996.

Taber, Jane. "Halifax's Waterfront Will Honour a Historic Sea Battle on Land." *The Globe and the Mail*, January 27, 2014.

Te Papa. "Teremoe." http://www.tepapa.govt.nz/Education/OnlineResources/SGR/Pages/Teremoe.aspx (accessed January 21, 2016).

The Tribune. "INS Viraat to Turn into a Museum." http://www.tribuneindia.com/news/nation/ins-viraat-to-turn-into-a-museum/102073.html (accessed August 18, 2015).

Titanic: World's Largest Museum Attraction. "Titanic Merchandise-Featured Items." https://www.titanicpigeonforge.com/cart_display.php?c=featured (accessed August 19, 2015).

Toland, John. "A Profile in Courage, a Background of War." *New York Times*, November 19, 1961.

United States Naval Academy. "Chaplain's Center." http://www.usna.edu/Chapel/virtualTour/crypt.php (accessed January 9, 2016).

United States Navy. "Welcome Aboard: The United States Navy Memorial and Naval Heritage Center." Brochure, Washington, D.C. (accessed July 25, 2015).

———. "Top Secret Report on German Prisoners Taken Aboard the USS *Block Island*, CVE 21, January 14, 1944 From U-231." U.S. Navy. USS Block Island Association Collection. San Diego, CA.

United States Navy Memorial Heritage Center. "Commemorative Plaque Wall." Informational Brochure, Washington, D.C. (accessed by author July 25, 2015).

———. "Welcome Aboard." Informational Brochure, Washington, D.C. (accessed by author July 25, 2015).

United States Postal Service. "Veterans and the Military on Stamps." http://about.usps.com/publications/pub528.pdf (accessed November 14, 2015).

University of Alaska Museum of the North. "Acquisitions and Accessioning." https://www.uaf.edu/museum/collections/ethno/policies/acquisitions (accessed August 25, 2015).

United States Naval Institute News. "World's Oldest Active Aircraft Carrier INS Viraat Set to Be Museum Ship in India." http://news.usni.org/2015/07/06/worlds-oldest-active-aircraft-carrier-ins-viraat-set-to-be-museum-ship-in-india (accessed August 18, 2015).

USS Gambier Bay (CVE 73). "Welcome to the Commissioning of USS George Washington, CVN 73." http://www.ussgambierbay-vc10.com/geoWashington.php (accessed January 26, 2012).

USS Franklin (CV 13). "The Ship That Wouldn't Die." http://www.ussfranklin.org (accessed November 14, 2011).

USS Pueblo (AGAR 2). "Background." http://www.usspueblo.org/index.html (accessed December 13, 2015).

USS Shipley Bay, CVE 85. "Aircraft Carrier Memorial." http://www.shipleybay.com/memorialacc.htm (accessed February 1, 2012).

USS St. Lo Association. "Ship History." http://www.ussstlo.com/contentPage.cfm?ID=455 (accessed January 23, 2012).

———. "The End of a Fighting Ship." http://www.ussstlo.com/contentPage.cfm?ID=414 (accessed January 23, 2012).

USS *Theodore Roosevelt*, CVN 71. "'Billy' the Moose and Theodore Roosevelt" exhibit panel. Norfolk, Virginia. Visited by author May 30, 2009.

Vachon, Ken. Personal correspondence dated March 28, 2007, Block Island Historical Society, Block Island, Rhode Island.

Vashon Loop. "Sxwobabc Exhibit Wins Awards." http://www.vashonloop.com/article/sxwobabc-exhibit-wins-awards (accessed January 15, 2016).

Vernetti, Hector. Interviewed by Ben Hruska, December 12, 2010, Tempe, Arizona.

Vineyard Gazette. "Whaleship Charles W. Morgan Arrives to Warm Welcome." "http://vineyard-gazette.com/news/2014/06/19/whaleship-charles-w-morgan-arrives-warm-welcome?k=vg-5622b276b14f1&r=1 (accessed October 17, 2015).

Walker, Dale L. *The Boys of 98: Theodore Roosevelt and the Rough Riders*. New York: Forge Book, 1998.

Whangaroa, Northland New Zealand. "Matauri Bay and the Cavalli Islands." http://www.whangaroa.co.nz/matauri-bay.cfm (accessed September 20, 2015).

World War II Database. "Battleship Yamato." http://ww2db.com/ship_spec.php?ship_id=1 (accessed November 8, 2015).

Y'Blood, William. *Hunter-Killer: U.S. Escort Carriers in the Battle of the Atlantic*. Annapolis, MD: Naval Institute Press, 1983.

YouTube. "La Belle Shipwreck." https://www.youtube.com/watch?v=zVd0-OOWSt0 (accessed September 2, 2015).

Index

About the Author

DR. BENJAMIN J. HRUSKA is a history instructor at Basis International School in Shenzhen, China. Before this, he served as the court historian for the Department of Defense's U.S. Court of Appeals for the Armed Forces in Washington, D.C. He completed his PhD in public history at Arizona State University in 2012. His dissertation focused on the actions of self-commemoration by U.S. Navy veterans in World War II. Before graduate school, he served as the executive director of a small maritime museum, the Block Island Historical Society on Block Island, Rhode Island. He earned an MA in public history from Wichita State University in 2004 and a BA in history from Pittsburg State University in 2000.